Preparing for the Classroom

Preparing for the Classroom

What Teachers Really Think about Teacher Education

Kevin O. Mason

ROWMAN & LITTLEFIELD
Lanham • Boulder • New York • London

Published by Rowman & Littlefield
A wholly owned subsidiary of The Rowman & Littlefield Publishing Group, Inc.
4501 Forbes Boulevard, Suite 200, Lanham, Maryland 20706
www.rowman.com

16 Carlisle Street, London W1D 3BT, United Kingdom

British Library Cataloguing in Publication Information Available

Library of Congress Cataloging-in-Publication Data Available

978-1-4758-0041-8 (cloth : alk. paper)
978-1-4758-0042-5 (pbk. : alk. paper)
978-1-4758-0043-2 (electronic)

♾️™ The paper used in this publication meets the minimum requirements of American National Standard for Information Sciences—Permanence of Paper for Printed Library Materials, ANSI/NISO Z39.48-1992.

Printed in the United States of America

Contents

Foreword

As teacher educators we often read criticisms of how educators are prepared in the United States—in conversations with friends, in conversations with policy makers, and in the press. In this book, Kevin Mason does something that should have been obvious to the profession for decades. He asks: What do teachers really think about teacher education? And to answer the question he asks the teachers! Now it is not uncommon for institutions to survey their graduates regarding their view of their experience, often in preparation for accreditation. But this is far more thorough and informative than one sees in reviewing efforts by colleges to begin to answer the question.

For one thing, he finds that there is often a significant gender gap, with women seeing their experience more positively than men. Is there something to be learned from this? Are we not serving future male teachers well? Some of his findings are not surprising, for example the study of classroom management is often seen as inadequate. Is the view based on an accurate perception or is it a reflection of the fear of beginning teaching? We have here data from teachers about their view of their own programs and teacher education as it exists now.

This is breakthrough research using mixed methods to inform teacher educators, the public, and policy makers. It gives colleges and universities a study to which their own results can be compared. It provides doctoral students, who are future teacher educators, insights into a line of research to be expanded upon, and it includes the actual surveys used in the study.

Teacher educators will find the work fascinating and useful. I think it could also be used with future educators to connect their own perceptions about their ongoing preparation with the views of practicing teachers.

This book needs to be read thoroughly, and is enhanced by profiles of teachers who participated in interviews. I suggest resisting the temptation to look at the author's summaries toward the end of the book before we do our own interpretations. Enjoy your explorations.

Nicholas M. Michelli
Presidential Professor of Teacher Education
Ph.D. Program in Urban Education
The City University of New York
New York, New York

Preface

The role of teacher education in society is of great importance. How we educate teachers and prepare them for the classroom and a lifetime of professional development has an enormous influence on society. I have appreciated the privilege and responsibility of being a teacher educator for the past eight years, after six years of teaching high school chemistry and physics. My career as a science teacher and teacher educator has allowed me to combine my passions for science, learning, and working with young people. I have found many rewards in pursuing a career that can positively affect so many people.

I believe what we do in education, in K–12 schools and in colleges and universities, is of the utmost importance. For this reason, I want to see teacher education accomplish its central purpose of preparing teachers to teach effectively and contribute positively to students' learning and overall development. As I progress through my professional career, I want to continue to improve my own practice and effectiveness as a teacher educator.

I firmly believe that those with teaching experience should be consulted and utilized in refining the curriculum and instruction of pre-service teacher education programs. Pre-service teacher education refers to the education that teachers experience prior to their initial certification and employment as a teacher. The involvement of practicing teachers and their ideas in the field of pre-service teacher education may provide new opportunities for teacher educators to learn about teaching and preparing pre-service teachers for both success and longevity in the classroom.

The views of practicing teachers should be actively pursued on a regular basis by researchers and teacher educators to inform how teacher educators prepare new teachers for the field of education. You don't learn to write novels by talking to engineers and you don't learn to design computers by talking to writers. Teachers need a voice in teacher education.

Although many teacher educators have experience teaching in K–12 schools, it is not enough to simply rely upon one's own experience or the experience of any one person. As a former teacher and current teacher educator, I know that practicing teachers in today's schools have many different perspectives on learning, teaching, and teacher education. Their perspectives and insights are based on their own experiences, which may differ from my own.

The views of practicing teachers are often grounded in a practical context and can provide a complement to the expertise of university researchers and teacher educators, who are often criticized for taking an overly theoretical approach to teacher education. In my conversations with teachers, I am constantly finding new ideas and motivations for working with pre-service teachers. These interactions with teachers can take the form of informal conversations or formal interviews, as was done in researching this book.

Currently, the study of practicing teachers and their ideas in pre-service teacher education is surprisingly uncommon in the research literature (Toll, Nierstheimer, Lenski, & Kolloff, 2004). I have no explanation or excuses for this lack of inquiry. As a teacher educator, I am both a part of the problem and solution. In this case, the dearth of studies on practicing teachers in teacher education presented an exciting new opportunity for study, exploration, and growth. That exploration has resulted in this book. It is my hope that this book encourages thought, discussion, and further study of teachers and teacher education.

1

A Voice for Teachers

In the hallways, classrooms, and teacher lounges of schools across America, teachers are sharing stories about pre-service teacher education. Each teacher's story is a personal recollection and evaluation of the university experiences that prepared them for the classroom. Each story is unique and distinctly different from the next. They differ because pre-service teacher education programs differ. The curriculum, instruction, and faculty create a unique set of experiences that varies from one university to the next.

They differ because teachers differ. Each future teacher enrolled in a pre-service teacher education program learns differently and benefits from the curriculum and instruction in varying ways and to varying extents. Some teachers were inspired to learn and grow by their pre-service teacher education experience and other teachers merely navigated the waters and avoided the obstacles necessary to reach their destination. The stories and perspectives of many teachers on a wide variety of topics in pre-service teacher education have been assembled in this book with the intent of providing a collective voice for teachers on pre-service teacher education that includes their praises, criticisms, and recommendations.

This book explores and examines many current practices, perceptions, issues, and concerns in pre-service teacher education through the lens of practicing teachers. What are the views of practicing teachers on the current issues facing pre-service teacher education? To answer this question, teachers were surveyed and interviewed on a wide variety of topics in pre-service teacher education with some expected and some surprising results.

The topics explored through the survey and interviews included the effectiveness of pre-service teacher education, the relevance of pre-service teacher education, and the influence of university methods courses on their teaching. The surveys and interviews also asked questions about a variety of trends and reforms in teacher education such as increased field experiences, professional development schools, standards-based teacher education, alternative certification, and others. The teachers' insights, based on their experiences in pre-service teacher education and the elementary or secondary classroom, may help to better prepare the next generation of teachers for success and longevity in the profession.

More importantly, their voices add a new perspective on the effectiveness and practicality of the current trends and reforms in pre-service teacher education. The teachers' perspective on pre-service teacher education is a valuable source of evidence and feedback, which can be utilized by those involved in pre-service teacher education to inform their work with pre-service teachers. This would include teacher educators as well as elementary and secondary teachers and administrators who work with pre-service teachers. In addition, the perspective of teachers must be considered along with other sources of evidence and reflection, such as educational philosophy, history, research, and theory.

Considering a new perspective on pre-service teacher education does not necessitate the elimination of other established perspectives and approaches to preparing teachers. In considering and reflecting on each perspective, the optimal approach to teacher preparation can be triangulated. This requires teachers and teacher educators to collaboratively reflect on their own experiences and the experiences of others. In short, teachers can be an important contributor to teacher education reforms.

Each chapter will examine a different set of topics in pre-service teacher education and discuss the teachers' perspective. Each topic is introduced at a level that is appropriate for novices in the field of teacher education, but, at the same time, offers insights that are valuable to experts as well. Teachers have their own experiences in teacher education, a professional interest in how new teachers are prepared for the classroom, and wisdom to share with the university professorate in education.

Despite the many complaints and criticisms often heard from individuals on the condition and status of pre-service teacher education, most teachers surveyed rated their own experience in pre-service teacher education as a positive one. On the other hand, teachers also expressed many concerns about pre-service teacher education and described some of the challenges for which they felt unprepared. Later, you will discover why some teachers were satisfied with pre-service teacher education while others were not. You will also learn what teachers recommended for improving the quality of pre-service teacher education.

Finally, in the latter chapters, you will be introduced to eight teachers who were interviewed by the author. These chapters tell a personal story and allow the teachers to explain, in their own words, the thoughts and reasoning behind the views expressed in the survey and discussed throughout the book. The common themes that emerged from these interviews reveal what teachers truly value in pre-service teacher education.

WHY STUDY TEACHER EDUCATION?

The phrase *teacher education* is used to refer to both pre-service and in-service education of teachers for the purposes of acquiring the knowledge, skills, and dispositions necessary for effective teaching. In-service teacher education refers to the education teachers receive after their initial certification and throughout their teaching careers. Teachers often join professional organizations, attend professional conferences, participate in teacher workshops, and complete graduate level degree programs as a part of their in-service teacher education. These activities are important, but not the focus of this book. Instead, this book will focus on the pre-service component of teacher education.

Pre-service teacher education refers to the education that teachers undergo prior to their initial certification and employment as a teacher. In most cases, this is accomplished by attending a university undergraduate degree program and graduating with a bachelor's degree in elementary or secondary education. In general, most teacher education programs are built from the same raw materials: general education courses, content courses, professional education courses, and field experiences.

Despite these similarities, there are many variations and exceptions across traditional undergraduate university pre-service teacher education programs. Studies have found that curricula and instruction in university pre-service teacher education programs vary widely in the United States (Grossman & Loeb, 2008). In addition, there are teachers who enter the classroom without ever attending a university undergraduate program.

A number of teachers also enter the teaching profession from alternative certification routes, which are often defined as anything other than the traditional university undergraduate preparation program. This includes university graduate programs that offer a master's degree for initial certification and other non-university alternative programs. These alternative certification programs vary tremendously in their design and delivery, even more than traditional pre-service teacher education.

These programs are often designed for college graduates or those entering the teaching profession from another profession to areas where teacher shortages may exist. The alternative programs often attract a unique audience of professionals to teaching, with varying credentials and experience. Alternative programs also commonly target a particular need, such as supplying teachers to urban schools or preparing teachers in subject areas with a critical shortage of teachers. Because of their unique audience and mission, the programs vary significantly.

Additionally, the job requirements for a teacher vary significantly from one school to the next. There really is no such thing as an American educational system. Each state and local region in the United States exerts control and influence over their own educational system; each local region also has a unique culture composed of diverse values, beliefs, and traditions. While most other countries form a centralized system of education, dictating the curriculum and instruction in each school, the United States offers a decentralized system, which emphasizes local control.

The variation in pre-service teacher education and K–12 schools across the United States makes the study of teacher education more challenging. Most studies tend to study only one program or model of pre-service teacher education. However, this study intends to collectively examine the views of teachers, who have graduated from a wide variety of pre-service teacher education programs. This variation results in many different perspectives, and each is important to informing the policies and practices of pre-service teacher education. We have much to learn from each other.

The passing of No Child Left Behind in 2001 brought greater attention to the issue of teacher quality and how teachers are prepared and licensed. This legislation required states and school districts to be accountable for placing a "highly qualified" teacher in every classroom. The notion of highly qualified and what that means became a prevalent topic in political and educational discourse in the years that followed. Typically, the discussion of highly qualified teachers was simplified to revolve around the licensing or certification of teachers. Those who were teaching without certification or outside of their certification area were deemed to be unqualified.

Although this may seem obvious to some, policy makers in most states allow the use of emergency certifications because of the teacher shortages that exist in some geographical areas and high need subject areas, like science, technology, math, and special education. If schools are unable to find a qualified candidate to fill a position, it can fill the position with an unqualified candidate, as long as the candidate is granted an emergency certification by the state. The emergency certification is temporary and often lasts for only one year.

This practice is a temporary solution to a permanent problem. Imagine the uproar if this approach was applied to other professions, like law or medicine. The issue is a challenge to the professional stature of teachers and No Child Left Behind, for all of its flaws and criticisms, was right to call attention to it. Nonetheless, the practice of granting emergency certifications has continued, and is quite common in certain areas and subjects. No Child Left Behind really just stated the obvious—there is a need for highly qualified teachers in every classroom.

However, in many discussions regarding highly qualified teachers, it seems that most presume that all certified teachers are well qualified and well prepared for the classroom. It is certainly easier to use a teacher's certifications as a measure of quality, but it says nothing of the teacher's effectiveness as a teacher or the implicit effectiveness of the teacher education program from which he or she graduated.

In 1996, the National Commission on Teaching and America's Future concluded that teacher quality and teacher education were the most significant factors in improving student achievement in U.S. schools. As a society, and especially as educators, we should demand a certified teacher in every classroom, but we should also aim past that goal. Why set the bar so low? We should strive to make improvements of varying magnitudes to the effectiveness of teacher education so that qualified teachers are better prepared for the rigors and challenges of the classroom, not merely certified to teach at a given grade level or subject area.

According to the 2009 U.S. Census, there are an estimated 3.6 million teachers and 55.2 million students in K–12 schools in the United States. Even small improvements in the effectiveness of pre-service teacher education can positively affect millions of teachers and students in the United States. To borrow from the field of psychology, we must achieve the principle of successive approximation, as we take steps toward a more effective and respected system of pre-service teacher education. Practicing teachers are a valuable asset and partner in that journey.

WHY ASK TEACHERS ABOUT TEACHER EDUCATION?

As teacher educators and others strive to improve teacher quality, we must recognize the value of stakeholder access and input from other educational professionals, including practitioners in the field. The reflective and data-driven approaches to continual improvement must not be driven by state or federal law, but rather from within teacher education. They must be inclusive and empowering to teacher education, rather than compliance-driven and punitive. There must be ongoing attempts to involve internal and external stakeholders in teacher education to celebrate our successes, identify our challenges, and respond to the needs of teachers in the field. To accomplish this, we must ask teachers.

In our discussion of pre-service teacher education, one very important question must be continually asked and addressed: How can the quality of pre-service teacher education be improved? There are countless thoughts and strategies that are being designed, considered, and employed to improve the effectiveness of teacher education. Unfortunately, many of the reforms in teacher education are influenced as much or moreso by political factors as professional factors. Sadly, teachers are not always engaged in the dialogue on this important issue for the teaching profession.

Some research suggests that the absence of teachers' voices may be a fatal flaw in pre-service teacher education reforms. Some researchers have concluded that the effectiveness of current university pre-service teacher education programs has been hampered by the gap between theory and practice. "Both of us find traditional models of teacher preparation inadequate, especially when schools and universities are separated as sites of theory and practice, or when schools and communities are disconnected as sites for student learning" (Boyle-Baise & McIntyre, 2008, p. 307).

Everyone has a stake in education and a right to contribute to the dialogue on what teachers should know and be able to do upon completion of their teacher preparation. Divergent opinions prevail across the local and national news, and in the legislative actions taken at the state and federal levels. Not all opinions are created equal, however, and not all voices are being heard.

The opinions of elected politicians and appointed officials appear especially prominent when it comes to many topics in education (Lee & Yarger, 1996). The voices of experts and researchers from colleges and universities are also influential, as they should be. The voice that is not commonly heard in the education literature on pre-service teacher education is the voice of practicing teachers (Toll, Nierstheimer, Lenski, & Kolloff, 2004).

WHY NOT ASK TEACHERS?

One argument that might be made against engaging teachers in a discussion on pre-service teacher education is the all too frequent criticism that today's schools and teachers are failing. Should teacher educators seek input from teachers in a failed system? Don't we need to move away from the current practices of teachers? There are several responses to such an argument.

First, despite the contemporary political rhetoric and media reports, the sky is not falling down on U.S. education. The student achievement level in many schools, both public and private, is remarkably high and compares favorably with other nations (Lehane, 2008). At the same time, some schools are not achieving critical success in student learning.

There is an achievement gap problem in the United States, which dwarfs the achievement gaps in other countries. There are enormous differences between the achievement of low-income and affluent students in the United States (Lehane, 2008). Schools with more low-income students significantly trail schools with affluent students on standardized measures of student achievement (Lehane, 2008).

In short, there is a poverty problem in the United States, which negatively affects learning and achievement for an increasing number of students. As the number of students in poverty increases in the United States, the national achievement scores on standardized exams decrease. Today, teachers and teacher educators are working tirelessly to offset and overcome these economic and familial challenges. This is one problem that must be addressed as a society; it may not be a reason to rebuke or condemn teachers or teacher educators.

There are many great qualities in American schools that other countries, even those with higher standardized exam scores, are studying and trying to emulate. The ability of our citizens to think, reason, and innovate is a testimony to our educational system and its teachers. The number of scholars, researchers, and Nobel Prize winners in the United States is evidence of an effective educational system. The number of advances in medicine, business, and industry that have emerged from those educated in the United States speaks volumes to how we educate our citizens. Our schools are not failing and neither are our teachers.

In many respects, these may be more authentic and meaningful measures than the exams used to compare students in reading, math, or science. If you replace standardized exams with more authentic outcome-based measures, our standing in international comparisons rises significantly and our schools and students look remarkably effective. Instead, we often measure what is easier to measure, rather than what is important. Preparing our students to innovate, collaborate, communicate, and use evidence to answer questions and solve problems is difficult to measure. Nonetheless, it should be a priority for our schools, teachers, and students.

Second, improving pre-service teacher education can be one of the most time and cost-effective approaches to improving student achievement. This approach can focus our efforts on hundreds of teacher education programs in the United States. Its potential to influence millions of students over the course of the next several decades would be significant and measurable. This is a good use of our educational dollars and resources.

Third, if we want to know how to better prepare new teachers for the challenges of teaching in today's schools, we must ask today's teachers and value their perspective. Teachers are aware of the obstacles that often impede their practice and student achievement in their classrooms, and are in a unique position to offer valuable wisdom and insight to teacher educators.

The lessons learned from teachers can help teacher educators to better prepare the next generation of teachers who may face similar conditions and challenges. The collective voice of teachers from the field offers those involved in preparing new teachers a new source of evidence to inform their practices. Teachers are a valuable partner and stakeholder in this endeavor.

2

Perspectives on Teacher Education

Researchers and teacher educators have the potential to amplify the voice of practicing teachers through published research in educational journals and the involvement of teachers in the process of pre-service teacher preparation. However, teacher educators and schools of education have faced many criticisms and challenges from both their university colleagues and the public, which have diminished their power and influence in the field of education.

In his book, *The Trouble with Ed Schools*, Labaree declared that schools of education are often considered "as low as you can go in the hierarchy of academic challenges" (2004, p. 2). Labaree attributed this low status, in part, to the historical origins of university-based teacher education (2004).

Clifford and Guthrie claimed that teacher educators only damaged their status further in their attempt to add academic credibility and build a larger body of research-based knowledge (1988). Clifford and Guthrie (1988) stated:

> They have seldom succeeded in satisfying the scholarly norms of their campus letters and science colleagues, and they are simultaneously estranged from their practicing professional peers. The more forcefully they have rowed toward the shores of scholarly research, the more distant they have become from the public schools they are duty bound to serve. (p. 3)

Schools of education are frequently criticized within the field of education by practicing teachers. According to Labaree, "teachers decry its programs as impractical and its research as irrelevant" (2004, p. 3). These challenges to the authority and status of teacher educators have made educational reforms difficult to implement and influence practice. Although teacher educators hold the keys to the educational research and reform engine, their reform efforts are often undermined by practitioners who are slow to accept and implement new ideas in curriculum and instruction.

In her book, *Inside Teaching*, Kennedy attempted to explain "why teachers seem to ignore the guidance offered to them by so many concerned groups" (2005, p. 1). Kennedy commented that "reform movements have come and gone for decades without much visible impact on teaching practices" (2005, p. 3). Kennedy identified five commonly cited explanations for the failure of reform efforts to influence teachers: teacher knowledge, teachers' beliefs, teachers' dispositions, circumstances in schools, and unrealistic reforms (2005, p. 12). Kennedy (2005) explained:

> Rarely do reformers think seriously about the array of real students and situations that teachers face in their classrooms. For the most part, the reform ideals also don't address the nitty-gritty problem of how to organize and manage learning in large groups, where managing the group can interfere with managing the ideas. (p. 18).

To test these explanations, Kennedy studied 45 teachers and observed 499 "episodes of teaching practice" (2005, p. 26). Her research confirmed that all five explanations contribute to the failure of reform ideals (Kennedy, 2005). Her research also highlighted some key differences that existed between teachers and reformers. In general, she found that "teachers are concerned about a broader range of issues than reformers" (Kennedy, 2005, p. 183). For example, Kennedy found that teachers were concerned about "the classroom as a community, their own personal needs, student willingness to participate, and lesson momentum" (2005, p. 183). Kennedy found that these issues were not typically considered by reformers (2005).

These differences between teachers and reformers help to explain the perceived gap between theory and practice in the field of education. It also provides an evidence-based argument for including practicing teachers and their ideas, in addition to the ideas of reformers and researchers, in pre-service teacher education. Namely, teachers will be able to bring a different set of beliefs and values about teaching that may contribute positively to the preparation of new teachers.

Labaree noted that efforts have been made in recent years to "narrow the gap between teacher and researcher" (2004, p. 92). These include movements to "encourage teachers to carry out research" as well as movements to "focus university research on issues of teacher practice in the classroom" (Labaree, 2004, p. 92). Labaree later stated, "One way to deal with the cultural divide between teachers and researchers is to acknowledge it explicitly and to sell teacher-students vigorously on the value of adopting the researcher perspective—as an addition to rather than replacement for the teacher perspective" (2004, p. 101).

The reverse may also be true. There may be value added to pre-service teacher education by acknowledging the divide explicitly and selling teacher educators on the value of adopting the teacher perspective as an addition to rather than replacement for the researcher perspective. Further research is needed on the effect of involving teachers and teachers' ideas in pre-service teacher education. Although there are a number of examples of teacher involvement cited in the field, the research base is still relatively small. Further research is needed to determine the effect and effectiveness of teacher involvement on preparing pre-service teachers for successful careers and contributions to students and the field of education.

Successful reforms in education and teacher education may depend on this type of mutual respect and acceptance of ideas, experiences, and perspectives. In this regard, collaboration is necessary to produce such results. Like the status of teacher educators, the status of teachers has been historically quite low (Kennedy, 2005). In order for their status and credibility to ascend, the two groups must accept their differences, embrace the expertise that each possesses, and begin working collaboratively in the classroom and at the university.

In a study of several teacher education programs, Tatto found that "in those few cases where faculty espoused more coherent views around professional norms, student teachers tended to show more definite movement toward developing views that were in turn congruent with those espoused by faculty" (1996, p. 175). Clifford and Guthrie recommended that teacher educators "must be made more cognizant of the technical or experiential culture of schooling" (1988, p. 349–50). Based on these findings, our knowledge and understanding of how teachers view teaching and teacher education must become a priority for all educators.

THE PERSPECTIVES OF TEACHERS AND TEACHER EDUCATORS

According to Labaree, the perceived theory-practice gap between teachers and teacher educators is an end result of two lenses or perspectives on teaching and learning (2004). Labaree argued that "teachers see things normatively researchers see things analytically" (2004, p. 95). Teachers highly value the artistic skill of practitioners as developed through experience and hope to improve upon their effectiveness in a particular setting and with a particular population of students. On the other hand, researchers examine the nature of teaching and learning scientifically and seek to find generalizability in their findings.

Practicing teachers and teacher educators practice and study their professions in two distinct worlds, each with its own culture, philosophy, and emphasis. The interaction and collaboration between these two worlds is often limited by the restraints of time and geography. The different cultures, and lack of interaction between them, have contributed to the construction of an artificial barrier between the art and the science of teaching.

University researchers study K–12 classrooms from the perspective of an observer, or temporary participant observer, while practicing teachers are essentially full-time participant observers. It is inevitable that these two perspectives will occasionally produce different observations and conclusions about teaching and learning. When the two views differ, the ideas endorsed in research journals and university classrooms are sometimes labeled as theory and often criticized by teachers as being impractical (Labaree, 2004).

Similarly, the ideas being traditionally and routinely implemented by practicing teachers are labeled as practice and often criticized by researchers as being out-dated or unsubstantiated (Labaree, 2004). It's not that the field of education has two distinct realities or forms. Rather, it is the position and experience of the observer that influences the observation and interpretation of the same event, in this case teaching and learning.

It is important to realize that making observations from two distinct frames of reference should be encouraged and can be advantageous to improving our understanding of the complex constructs of teaching and learning. However, it is only valuable when the two perspectives are mutually represented and respected in the professional literature. This requires that teachers and teacher educators interact and collaborate more than ever before. As their perspectives are shared, the dichotomy of theory and practice will become less pronounced and the art and science of teaching and learning to teach will be more cohesive and complementary.

The ideas of teachers and teacher educators on topics in education are not isolated entities. The work of university educators often reflect, analyze, and evaluate the work of teachers. Through the medium of educational research and professional journals, there has been a great deal of published observation and commentary from university researchers about the methods and effectiveness of teachers' practices. However, the reverse is typically not true. Teachers work in an environment that often does not provide the time, resources, or opportunity to contribute to the academic literature or comment on the practices of pre-service teacher education.

The exchange of ideas between teachers and teacher educators in the research literature is drastically asymmetrical. This asymmetry has hindered efforts to establish a more collaborative relationship between teachers and teacher educators. To address this concern, this book attempts to invite teachers into the pre-service teacher education discussion and debate by investigating the views of practicing teachers on a variety of issues.

Practicing teachers have learned to balance the theoretical knowledge of learning with the practical constraints of the classroom environment through experience. Those experiences are valuable in many ways. The lack of practicing teachers' voices in pre-service teacher education is detrimental to preparing future teachers for the challenges they will face in the classroom.

In the *Handbook of Research on Teacher Education*, Westheimer suggested that "shared decision-making, collective action regarding school policies, and reflection on broader school reform issues are seen as promising ways to engage teachers, foster collegiality, and improve practice" (2008, p. 764). Teachers' ideas can be used to inform the practice of teacher educators and revise the curriculum and instruction of pre-service teacher education. The views of practicing teachers provide invaluable feedback for everyone in the profession of teaching.

Pre-service teacher education programs have a responsibility to offer university experiences where students can develop the necessary theoretical and practical knowledge to make a successful start as a teacher as well as foster continued professional growth. To accomplish this task, teacher educators need to have one hand on the pulse of current educational research and the other on the pulse of practicing teachers. The optimal balance between the art and science of teaching or between the theory and practice of education may be difficult to pinpoint, but the shortage of one or the other will surely doom the noble attempts of teacher educators.

This should not be perceived as a balancing act where theory and practice are positioned on opposite ends of some sort of educational teetertotter. Rather, it is better compared to the balance of flavors in cooking, the balance of colors in decorating, or the balance of individual priorities in a relationship. It is about blending one into the other so well that we forget that the individual parts were ever separate entities. In this case, the concepts of theory and practice should be so perfectly blended in pre-service teacher education that we lose the notion of a dichotomy.

A CONSTRUCTIVIST PERSPECTIVE ON TEACHER EDUCATION

This book will study, discuss, and represent the views of practicing teachers on pre-service teacher education based upon the results of surveys and interviews with middle and secondary teachers from the state of Wisconsin. To study the views of teachers on various topics in pre-service teacher education, one must realize that teachers have constructed their own viewpoints and understandings about pre-service teacher education based on their unique experiences as pre-service and in-service teachers.

As a researcher and author, I will be constructing a representation of their views about pre-service teacher education based upon the data collected in the survey and interviews and sharing that representation with the readers of this book. For this reason, it is constructivism that is truly the cornerstone or the theoretical framework for the research and writing of this book.

Constructivism is a theory of teaching and learning that asserts that learners construct their own knowledge and understanding of the world around them (Gordon, 2008). Inside and outside of the classroom, students' understandings of history, science, or any other subject matter are built from their own ideas, the ideas of others, and their experiences. A student's mind does not simply store information like a computer and teachers do not simply transfer or download the information to the students. Learning takes place everywhere and prior knowledge, whether right or wrong, is mixed into the foundation as new learning and understandings are built upon it.

When constructivism is applied to teacher education, pre-service teachers, in-service teachers, and teacher educators may all assume the role of the learner at various times. Pre-service teachers, in-service teachers, and teacher educators are all constructing knowledge of how learning takes place based upon their own experiences in their own environments. Pre-service teachers learn from their experiences as students in K–12 classrooms, their experiences in university classrooms, and their experiences during their pre-student teaching and student teaching field experiences.

The pre-service teachers' understandings of how their students learn and how they can most effectively teach are constructed based upon each of these experiences. Each pre-service teacher may construct a slightly or vastly different understanding of learning and teaching. Indeed, there will be some similarities between the views of different pre-service teachers on the art and science of teaching.

After all, many pre-service teachers have learned about some of the same established educational philosophies and evidenced-based practices in the field of education. However, there will also be definite differences based upon the varied experiences and interpretation of those ideas and experiences by each individual pre-service teacher. Like snowflakes, each pre-service teacher's understanding of teaching and learning will be unique.

In the same way, in-service teachers have continued to build upon their earlier views of learning and teaching based upon their continued experiences in the classroom. In addition, their understanding of learning and teaching can be further built, modified, or even reconstructed in continuing education or professional development. Teachers' understanding of how students learn and how to best teach their students continues to grow and evolve throughout their teaching career.

In the same way, teacher educators are also constructing knowledge about learning and teaching during their experiences in graduate education, teaching in university classrooms, conducting professional research, and interacting with K–12 teachers. Teacher educators must then thoughtfully apply their understanding of learning and teaching to the curriculum and instruction of pre-service teacher education. The faculty of a university pre-service teacher education program must make hundreds or thousands of decisions that will significantly affect the education of pre-service teachers at the university.

Based upon a constructivist view of pre-service teacher education, it is critically important for teacher educators to recognize, study, and understand the knowledge and experiences of pre-service and in-service teachers. One of the unique attributes of a constructivist view of learning is the emphasis that it places on the prior knowledge and experiences of the learner.

In a constructivist paradigm, the existing ideas of the learner greatly influence the process and outcomes of learning. The prior knowledge and ideas of pre-service teachers will play a significant role in the learning that takes place during pre-service teacher education. Likewise, the prior knowledge and ideas of in-service teachers will play a significant role in the learning that takes place during in-service teacher education.

Finally, the ideas of in-service teachers may also contribute to pre-service teacher education as their experiences, wisdom, and insights are shared with teacher educators and pre-service teachers. From a constructivist perspective, it is also vitally important for teacher educators to understand how teachers continue to construct, modify, and apply their knowledge and understanding of teaching and learning throughout their teaching career. Teachers' understanding of teaching and learning based upon their experiences in the classroom could be extremely valuable to teacher educators in preparing pre-service teachers for similar classroom environments.

The *Handbook of Qualitative Research* stated that "constructivism connects action to praxis and builds on antifoundational arguments while encouraging experimental and multivoiced texts" (Denzin & Lincoln, 2000, p. 158). This view that learning is an active pursuit based upon many varied experiences is a common characteristic of constructivist teaching and learning (Gordon, 2008). Every individual who is involved in education and teacher education has constructed a valuable understanding and insight based upon their own unique set of experiences.

Practicing teachers have experienced pre-service teacher education, in-service teacher education, and their own classrooms. They have constructed a knowledge and understanding of the teaching profession based upon these experiences that may be unique from other educational professionals. Research conducted from a constructivist perspective encourages a "multivoiced" approach to educational research (Denzin & Lincoln, 2000, p. 158).

In research on teacher education, one of those voices should be that of practicing teachers. This book is really an attempt to bring the constructed knowledge and ideas of practicing teachers into the forefront of pre-service teacher education and encourage others in the field of teacher education to do the same. The construction of knowledge and practice in teacher preparation is a continual process of thoughtful reflection and purposeful action.

A RESEARCHER'S PERSPECTIVE ON TEACHER EDUCATION

There is a great deal of research being conducted in pre-service teacher education from a variety of ideological and theoretical perspectives. The research in pre-service teacher education employs a variety of research methods, both qualitative and quantitative. In the *Handbook of Research on Teacher Education*, Lee and Yarger wrote, "Much of teacher education research conducted at higher education institutions concerns the performance of teacher education programs, teacher educators, and/or teacher education students" (1996, p. 17).

The use of pre-service teachers as research subjects in the study of teacher education is quite common. It is a convenient sample to study for teacher educators and provides valuable data and insights into the effectiveness of teacher education and teacher education reforms. These research opportunities may be conducted as informal research to inform one's own practice or as formal research to publish and disseminate to others in academic journals. Pre-service teachers enrolled in university teacher education programs may be observed, surveyed, or interviewed, which provides valuable data for teacher educators to reflect upon and use to improve pre-service teacher education.

As a whole, researchers have been able to learn a great many things from this type of research, but it also has its limitations. First, many of the studies conducted in the past twenty years are case studies of a specific pre-service teacher education program and its effect on a small number of pre-service teachers. Because pre-service teacher education varies widely across the United States and from program to program, the findings of the individual case studies are often difficult to generalize.

Second, although this type of research can be very valuable, some researchers question its objectivity. Wilson, Floden, and Ferrini-Mundy cautioned, "Because much of the in-depth research is done locally by teacher educators who have an investment in the enterprise, results are sometimes suspect" (2002, p. 194). The researcher is often performing a study of the pre-service teacher education program at their own university using themselves, their colleagues, and their education students as participants.

This level of involvement and connection to the participants may lend itself to greater researcher bias. When studying one's own pre-service teacher education program, it is much more likely that researchers have preconceived notions of what they will see and what they will learn from the research. These preconceptions may influence the observations, analysis, and conclusions of the study.

A third limitation of research on pre-service teachers is that the studies do not track the development and evolution of teachers' knowledge, skills, and dispositions beyond graduation. This is incongruent with the view that learning to teach is a lifelong process where knowledge and skills continue to be developed throughout a teaching career.

If pre-service teacher education is meant to prepare teachers for continued learning as a teacher, the success or failure of pre-service teacher education programs and strategies should not be measured by the immediate progress of pre-service teachers prior to graduation. Rather, it is imperative that the body of research on pre-service teacher education also include the study of in-service teachers who are further along in their teaching careers.

In research on teacher education, the study of in-service teachers has been much less common than the study of pre-service teachers. A search of the research literature found only three research studies that investigated the views of in-service teachers on pre-service teacher education and only one that involved teachers with more than three years of teaching experience. Interestingly, the search for literature also found one study that investigated the views of middle school students on pre-service teacher education (Storz, 2003). The article discussed what future teachers must be prepared to encounter to effectively teach in a middle school classroom from the perspective of middle school students (Storz, 2003).

This article was fascinating in several regards. First, it provides a student perspective on what teachers should know and be able to do. Although it is not an expert opinion, it was interesting to read what students valued about teachers. Second, it demonstrated the value placed on student feedback in the field of education.

However, if the knowledge of middle school students is consulted in the research literature, how much more valuable and prolific should the practice of consulting in-service teachers be in the research literature on pre-service teacher education? Certainly experienced teachers possess knowledge and insight into teaching and teacher education that could be quite helpful to the future direction of pre-service teacher education.

There were three notable research studies that investigated the views of in-service teachers on pre-service teacher education. In the first study, Greenwood followed the development and progress of three teachers from the time they were pre-service teachers until three years after their completion of the teacher education program (2003). The teachers were enrolled in the one-year master of education program for second-career teachers at the University of Massachusetts at Lowell.

At the conclusion of the program, all the teachers were asked to complete an evaluation of the methods course. Greenwood noted that the evaluations from the three career-changing teachers were "extremely positive and many noted that they were not aware of the importance of working with (and not ignoring) students' ideas" (Greenwood, 2003, p. 220).

During their third year of teaching, the same three teachers were given a questionnaire and interviewed. In response to a question about what would have helped the teachers in their first year of teaching, one teacher cited the "need to know more about dealing with misbehavior, understanding adolescents, and learning problems" (Greenwood, 2003, p. 221). Another teacher also expressed a need for "more assistance with discipline problems" (Greenwood, 2003, p. 223). Finally, a third teacher had a long list of topics that he felt needed more coverage such as "discipline problems, learning problems, the nature of the adolescent, activities to engage students, better understanding of inquiry and a wider knowledge of how to teach each physics topic" (Greenwood, 2003, p. 225).

From the questionnaires and interviews, the researcher determined that two of the three teachers did in fact use many of the ideas emphasized in the methods course. Greenwood credited the study of teachers during their third year of teaching, rather than during their pre-service experience alone, for producing a "more viable representations of the link between beliefs and practice" (Greenwood, 2003, p. 230).

A second research study followed ten beginning teachers, five primary and five secondary teachers, in a longitudinal study from their final year of pre-service education through their third year of teaching (Grossman, Valencia, Evans, Thompson, Martin, & Place, 2000). The researchers utilized field observations and interviews to assess the influence of the pre-service teacher education courses on teaching strategies for literacy and writing. They found that all ten teachers used at least a portion of the techniques and strategies that had been emphasized in the pre-service teacher education program (Grossman, Valencia, Evans, Thompson, Martin, & Place, 2000).

The teaching strategies included the emphasis of ownership of writing, scaffolding of support and instruction, the use of writing workshops, and a focus on the process of writing rather than the product (Grossman, Valencia, Evans, Thompson, Martin, & Place, 2000). The results indicated that those techniques that were "buttressed with practical strategies" were even more influential on the future teaching practices of the teachers (Grossman, Valencia, Evans, Thompson, Martin, & Place, 2000, p. 631). This suggests that pre-service teachers would benefit from teacher preparation with a greater focus on practical contexts and applications.

The evidence of instructional strategies emphasized in the university coursework used in the lessons of the teachers became increasingly apparent in the second year of teaching (Grossman, Valencia, Evans, Thompson, Martin, & Place, 2000). The researchers also found that the curriculum materials used in the K–12 classroom also had a considerable amount of influence on the teaching strategies implemented by the teachers in the first year of teaching (Grossman, Valencia, Evans, Thompson, Martin, & Place, 2000).

In the second year of teaching, the teachers began to "critique and repair curriculum materials" more frequently before using them in their lessons (Grossman, Valencia, Evans, Thompson, Martin, & Place, 2000, p. 656). Based on this evidence, the authors warned other researchers about the "dangers of making claims about what teachers do and do not learn during teacher education based only on data from their 1st year of teaching" (Grossman, Valencia, Evans, Thompson, Martin, & Place, 2000, p. 631).

A third research study examined the views of eighteen in-service teachers on the characteristics necessary for becoming an effective physical education teacher (McCullick, 2001). As he analyzed the existing research on physical education teacher education (PETE), McCullick concluded that "one voice is missing; that of the practitioner" (2001, p. 36). McCullick stated that one of his intentions in this study was to give a "voice to those who teach physical education in an area in which they should be intimately familiar—the preparation of a teacher for public school" (2001, p. 35).

Unlike the two previous examples, this research involved in-service teachers with an average of 14.5 years of teaching experience (McCullick, 2001). In the study, each of the teachers was interviewed in a semi-structured interview which was audiotaped and later transcribed. From the data, four themes emerged about the characteristics that practicing teachers deemed necessary for future physical education teachers: a love of physical activity, physical fitness, a love of children and adolescents, and professional flexibility (McCullick, 2001).

In addition, the practicing teachers were asked about the traits that would be desirable in teacher education faculty. The study found three themes for the desirable qualities of teacher education faculty: credibility, a love of physical education, and a concern for their students (McCullick, 2001). In defining credibility, the teachers often alluded to teacher educators' level of K–12 teaching experience and knowledge of current issues in K–12 classrooms (McCullick, 2001).

Furthermore, eight of the eighteen teachers interviewed suggested that it would be beneficial for teacher educators to periodically return to K–12 schools to teach a class in the public schools in order to stay in touch with current issues (McCullick, 2001). The similarity of the characteristics for teacher educators and future teachers that emerged from the data also reaffirmed the importance of modeling in pre-service teacher education. Finally, the interviews also revealed that in-service teachers viewed the role of teacher educator as very important to the field of education and the professional development of pre-service teachers (McCullick, 2001).

Researchers in the field of teacher education have noted that "most research stops with student teaching; a few studies follow teachers into the first year of teaching; fewer still examine how teachers' understanding and practice evolve in the second and third year of practice" (Grossman, Valencia, Evans, Thompson, Martin, & Place, 2000, p. 632). One reason for the predominance of studies on pre-service teachers and recent graduates is the convenience of studying a sample that is currently or has been recently enrolled in the pre-service teacher education program at the researchers' university.

However, if teacher education has the objective of producing a lifelong effect on the careers of teachers, then in-service teachers with many years of experience must be involved in the research on pre-service teacher education. Doing so will allow researchers to better understand the lasting effects of pre-service teacher education programs and to include the practical ideas and strategies from teachers to inform the practice of teacher educators.

A PRACTITIONER'S PERSPECTIVE ON TEACHER EDUCATION

In his book *The Sources of a Science of Education*, Dewey expressed concern about the status and direction of educational research and its tendency to stray away from matters related to classroom teaching (1929). He foresaw a growing disconnect between theory and practice and called the educational research of the time "an arm chair science" (Dewey, 1929). Dewey's writing foreshadowed a concern that continues today.

In her review of educational research, Lagemann commented on Dewey's portrayal of educational research and stated, "Despite the new directions of recent years, those problems have remained central until century's end" (2000, p. 232). According to Lagemann, "Since the earliest days of university sponsorship, education research has been demeaned by scholars in other fields, ignored by practitioners, and alternatively spoofed and criticized by politicians, policy makers, and members of the public at large" (2000, p. 232).

As subjects of educational research, teachers have been analyzed and critiqued based upon a vast set of professional behaviors and expectations: planning, preparation, instruction, questioning, interactions with students, and many others. They have often been studied as research subjects, but much less frequently consulted for the knowledge and insight they possess as a result of their classroom experiences.

The activities of teaching and learning appear simple enough, but are extraordinarily complex and multifaceted. Each teacher and learner performs their respective functions with a complex combination of habits, routines, strategies, and styles. To understand something so complicated and varied understandably requires the ongoing study of teachers and students as subjects of research.

This type of teacher involvement as the subjects of educational research does not necessarily recognize or value the sizeable expertise of the teacher. It also does not necessarily allow teachers to be intellectual contributors to the research. There is no doubt teachers will continue to be the subjects of educational research, but they should also be intellectual contributors as well. Whether acting as researchers or participants, teachers have expertise and experience to share and contribute to educational research, including the study of pre-service teacher education.

The contributions of teachers as researchers may be incredibly valuable, but also has a significant limitation. Namely, teachers are not provided with time in their school day to perform research and other scholarly activity. Labaree (2004) commented on this limitation.

> A university faculty position gives professors the time and space to do research, sets expectations for the frequency and quality of research output, and enforces these expectations with pay and promotion incentives. None of these conditions is present in the position of the classroom teacher. (p. 96)

Cochran-Smith and Lytle found that teachers are reluctant to conduct research because of the amount of time it takes away from working with students (1992). This does not diminish the value of teachers' contributions to the research literature, but does limit the pervasiveness of teachers as researchers.

Therefore, when discussing the potential contributions of teachers to the research on pre-service teacher education, it is important to consider their potential contributions as research participants as well. As participants, teachers can provide sources of experience, knowledge, and expertise in all types of educational research. Research that utilizes and analyzes teacher expertise can make valuable contributions to the field of teacher education that will help inform decisions made by teacher educators regarding what is taught and learned in pre-service teacher education and how it is taught and learned.

Because most research in teacher education involves pre-service teachers, we tend to consider only the short-term effects of pre-service teacher education on teachers. Although practicing teachers are often involved in university teacher education as cooperating teachers or graduate students, their ideas are underrepresented in the literature on pre-service teacher education (Toll, Nierstheimer, Lenski, & Kolloff, 2004).

Lee and Yarger argued that "considering that teacher education is about teachers and teaching, researchers have much to learn from teachers about teaching" (1996, p. 33). The knowledge and understanding of learning and teaching that practicing teachers have constructed should be studied and shared with other educational professionals. It is quite reasonable for teacher educators to ask in-service teachers to reflect on their pre-service preparation and its effectiveness in preparing them for the classroom.

The current lack of research of this type in the literature provides an opportunity for this book to make a unique contribution. This book will attempt to seek out and listen to the voices of practicing teachers on the issues in pre-service teacher education. The lessons learned from this study may be able to add a new perspective on the effectiveness and potential reform of pre-service teacher education.

3

Talking with Teachers about Teacher Education

For this book, teachers were surveyed and interviewed about their views on pre-service teacher education. The use of both survey and interview methodologies was intended to improve the reliability and validity of the findings. The use of two research methodologies allows for the triangulation of data. In essence, it allows the researcher to view the same phenomena from two different viewpoints or frames of reference. The survey provided a quantitative lens to determine, as the title of this book suggests, what teachers really think about pre-service teacher education. The survey methodology allowed for a greater sample size so the results, in this case the views of teachers, could be better generalized to a larger population of teachers.

The interviews, on the other hand, provided a qualitative lens to explore the views of a smaller sample of in-service teachers in more depth. The interviews allowed for the teachers to answer the why and how questions that can be difficult to address in a survey. In essence, it allowed for teachers to explain the thoughts and reasoning behind the views that were expressed in the survey. It also allowed the researcher an opportunity to ask follow-up questions, when needed. When combined, these two methods complemented one another so that this book could better examine and represent the views of teachers on teacher education.

THE SURVEY

The survey was composed of thirty-seven questions covering a variety of issues in pre-service teacher education. First, it asked teachers about their own experiences in pre-service teacher education, including their thoughts on the effectiveness, relevance, influence, and gaps in preparation they experienced. There were also several open-ended questions, which allowed teachers to share their satisfactions, dissatisfactions, and recommendations. A copy of the survey instrument is located in appendix A, and the survey data are provided in appendix C.

Unlike many research studies that ask recent graduates to reflect on their teacher education experience, the teachers in this study had the advantages of experience and hindsight in reflecting on their own pre-service preparation. The disadvantage to this approach is that the teachers would not be as likely to remember details of their pre-service teacher education. Therefore, the survey questions did not ask for specific details about their experience, but focused instead on the teachers' overall impressions or thoughts on the program.

Second, the survey also asked teachers about their views on current pre-service teacher education. The majority of the teachers surveyed had worked with student teachers as a cooperating teacher and were at least somewhat informed on the practices of their local pre-service teacher education program. In the survey, the teachers expressed their satisfactions, concerns, and opinions on the current state of pre-service teacher education. They also provided their opinion on current issues such as standards-based teacher education, professional development school partnerships, and alternative certification programs for teacher licensure.

Finally, the teachers were asked about what they thought should be changed about pre-service teacher education. These recommendations are discussed in chapter 6 of the book. This was probably the most valuable feedback received from the teachers. Based on their experiences as practitioners, the teachers offered recommendations for both the field experience and university-based components of pre-service teacher education. They also had recommendations for expanding the role of in-service teachers in pre-service teacher education and the desired qualifications of teacher educators. A copy of the survey can be found in appendix A.

THE SURVEY SAMPLE

The survey sample was randomly selected from a list of middle and high school teachers in the state of Wisconsin available through the Wisconsin Department of Public Instruction (DPI). Although the teachers on the list were licensed middle and high school teachers, some of the teachers who responded indicated that they teach at the elementary level. The random selection of the sample was the best approach for producing results that are generalizable to the larger population of Wisconsin middle and high school teachers. Although this study was conducted with Wisconsin teachers, the results and conclusions may be of interest and importance to teachers and teacher educators everywhere.

The survey was sent to 1,000 teachers from the state of Wisconsin and 191 teachers responded. This sample size (191) and response rate (19.1 percent) resulted in a confidence level of 95 percent and margin of error of 7.1 percent for the survey results. For the purposes of understanding how teachers perceive pre-service teacher education, this was considered more than sufficient.

The race, gender, and age of the survey participants were obtained along with other background characteristics of the respondents, including the years of teaching experience, grade level taught, subject area taught, and number of graduate credits. These background characteristics provided a valuable description of the survey sample. It also led to some interesting discoveries about the differences of teachers' views, based on these demographic factors. A summary description of the survey sample is given below in table 3.1.

In general the survey sample was a mostly Caucasian group of teachers with an average age of forty-three years and an average of seventeen years of teaching experience. The survey sample included male (41 percent) and female (59 percent) who taught a wide variety of subjects, mostly at the middle and high school level. You will also notice in table 3.1 that the teachers in the survey sample had completed an average of forty-one credits beyond their bachelor's degree. In fact, the majority of the survey sample had completed a master's degree (figure 3.1), which indicates a very well-educated survey sample.

Table 3.1. Description of the Teachers Surveyed

Race	Gender	Age (Years)	Experience (Years)	Grade Level	Subject Area	Graduate Credits
96% Caucasian	59% Female	Average of 43	Average of 17	3% K-5	18% Multiple	Average of 41
0.5% Asian	41% Male	Std Dev of 11	Std Dev of 11	5% K-8	16% English	Std Dev of 23
0.5% Hispanic		Range of 24 to 65	Range of 1 to 43	26% 6-8	16% Math	Range of 0 to 156
1% Other				16% 6-12	11% Science	
2% Unknown				49% 9-12	11% Social	
				2% Unknown	29% Other	

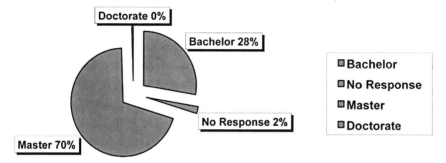

Figure 3.1. Highest Degree Earned by Survey Sample of Teachers

THE INTERVIEW

Although the survey was effective in examining the views of teachers, it did not provide the depth of understanding to explain why teachers might hold certain views of pre-service teacher education. To better understand the reasoning behind teachers' views on pre-service teacher education, interviews were conducted with a portion of the survey sample. The interview explored and explained many of the topics addressed in the survey. A copy of the interview instrument can be found in appendix B.

The interview consisted of twenty-seven questions written by the author and reviewed by other experts in the field of teacher education. Occasionally, the author asked additional questions to follow-up on the ideas expressed by the teacher being interviewed. The semi-structured interview format allowed teachers to further explain their thoughts and reasoning behind the views expressed in the survey and provided a second method of data collection to triangulate the research findings and improve the reliability of the conclusions. This format also allowed the teachers interviewed to discuss issues that may not have been addressed in the survey.

THE INTERVIEW SAMPLE

Eight teachers from the survey sample were interviewed. It was a purposive sample, meaning the teachers were selected for a specific reason or purpose. In this case, the interviewees were selected to represent a certain perspective expressed by multiple respondents in the survey. A factor analysis of the survey data was used to identify the different perspectives held by teachers. A factor analysis of the survey data identified a total of twenty-three different factors. A loading factor of 0.300 was used to remove extraneous variables and an eigenvalue was calculated for each factor. There were seven statistically significant factors with an eigenvalue greater than one.

For the purposes of creating the interview sample, the two factors with the largest eigenvalues were selected. The first factor was the teacher's level of satisfaction or dissatisfaction with their own pre-service teacher education experience. The second factor was the willingness of teachers to be involved in teacher education. Based on these two factors, the teachers in the survey sample could be divided into four groups or types of teachers.

The first group included those teachers who were generally satisfied with their pre-service teacher education experience and willing to become involved. The second group included those teachers who were satisfied with their pre-service teacher education experience, but unwilling to become involved. The third group included those teachers that were dissatisfied with their teacher education experience, but willing to become involved. Finally, the fourth group included those teachers who were generally dissatisfied with their pre-service teacher education experience yet were unwilling to become involved.

The four groups or types of teachers, along with pseudonyms for the eight teachers in the interview sample, are shown in table 3.2. Two teachers were selected to be interviewed from each group, resulting in a total of eight teachers. These eight teachers were contacted for an interview. One teacher respectfully declined the interview and was replaced by another

Table 3.2.   Four Groups of Teachers

	Satisfied with Their Teacher Education Experience	Dissatisfied with Their Teacher Education Experience
Willing to be Involved	Ms. Foster	Mr. Gray
	Ms. Wallace	Ms. Kraft
Unwilling to be Involved	Mr. Clark	Mr. Ford
	Mr. Cook	Ms. Nelson

randomly selected teacher from the same group. A second teacher did not respond after six attempts to contact them by phone and email and was replaced by another randomly selected teacher from the same category.

The teachers within the same group responded very similarly on the survey to a variety of different questions. As a result, interviewing several teachers from each group ensured that different ideas and perspectives found in the survey responses would be represented in the interview sample. You will meet all eight of these teachers and learn more about their perspectives on pre-service teacher education later in this book.

4

What Teachers Really Think about Their Teacher Education Experience

The purpose of this book was to discover what teachers really think about teacher education. The survey was intended to explore and examine the views of practicing teachers on a wide variety of topics and issues in pre-service teacher education. In the survey, teachers were asked to rate their own pre-service teacher education experience. The interview provided an opportunity to explore the same topics in more depth and learn about the reasoning behind each view expressed in the survey. This mixed methodology provided a more complete picture of teachers' perceptions of teacher preparation, including their own experiences and the state of current pre-service teacher education.

This chapter will focus on what teachers thought about the overall effectiveness of their own pre-service teacher education experience. What did these teachers really think about their own preparation? Was it effective? Was it relevant? What influence did it have on their teaching? What gaps did they have in their preparation for the teaching profession? These questions and more will be answered in this chapter.

EFFECTIVENESS

Despite the many complaints and criticisms often heard from individuals on the condition and status of pre-service teacher education, most teachers rated their own experience as a positive one. Four out of five teachers (79 percent) indicated that their pre-service teacher education experience was either good (31 percent), very good (30 percent), or excellent (18 percent). The complete report of the survey results can be found in appendix C.

Interestingly, there was a significant difference in how men and women rated their own experience in pre-service teacher education. In general, female teachers rated their pre-service teacher education experience significantly higher than males. Female teachers reported a mean score of 3.57 on a five point scale, while male teachers reported a mean score of 3.14 on a five point scale. Although this may not seem like a large difference, it was statistically significant ($t(185) = 1.45$, $p < 0.01$).

Historically, teaching has always been a female dominated profession. According to the National Center for Education Statistics, 76 percent of public school teachers are female (NCES, 2008). It is possible that the approaches taken to prepare teachers have been oriented toward females. Is there a bias against men in teacher education? In the same way that university preparation programs in science, technology, engineering, and mathematics (STEM) may unknowingly convey a bias against women, there may be a hidden bias against men in the field of teacher education. If you think this gender difference was just a fluke, just wait until the next chapter.

While the need for more women in the STEM fields is well documented and researched, the same cannot be said about men in education. The recruitment, retention, and support of women in STEM fields has been researched and supported through grant dollars, scholarships, or specialized programs. The recruitment, retention, and support of men entering the field of education has not been acted upon in the same way, perhaps because men are not usually considered to be an underrepresented population. In education, however, men are an underrepresented population.

Although the research does not exist to offer a clear explanation for the gender difference found in this survey, the gender difference is undeniable. Based on the results of this survey, there is clearly something about teacher education that appears to meet the needs of women to a greater degree than men. This may require more study and action on the part of researchers and teacher educators.

There is a need for future research to explore the potential gender bias in teacher education. In addition, there is a need to recruit, retain, and support more men entering the field of education. With the decline of the two parent household, often caused by an absent father, male teachers have a vital role to play in the sociological development of school-aged children, both boys and girls.

RELEVANCE

The most common criticism of pre-service teacher education is the "'ivory tower' nature of university faculty's perspective on how schools operate and what K–12 students are like" (Book, 1996, p. 207). The adage goes that teacher educators lack the experience and continued contact with K–12 students and teachers, and therefore, the curriculum and instruction designed for pre-service teachers is overly theoretical. Like many public perceptions, this belief has a historical context, an ounce of truth, and a pound of exaggeration.

Historically, the early courses in education at the university level during the mid-1800s were often taught by faculty members from other related fields of study, such as philosophy, psychology, and sociology (Lucas, 1996). Although these faculty members did not possess experience at the elementary or secondary level, they had expertise that was very useful for teachers. The expertise of the faculty greatly influenced the curriculum and instruction of early teacher preparation programs.

There is another reason faculty members in philosophy, psychology, and sociology were chosen as early teacher educators at the university. When courses and departments in curriculum and instruction first began to appear at the university during the nineteenth century, they were already employed by the university. As a result, the early courses and programs in education offered at the university level had a reputation for addressing the philosophy, psychology, and sociology of schools, with less attention to the practical application of pedagogy (Lucas, 1996).

Today, the situation is quite different. While the disciplines of philosophy, psychology, and sociology are still prominent in teacher education, teacher educators do generally have past experience working outside of the university, frequently in K–12 schools. A study by the National Center for Education Statistics found that 75 percent of university education faculty members had been employed outside the university and 68 percent of those had their first job in elementary or secondary schools (NCES, 1999). Nonetheless, the criticism that teacher education is overly theoretical and often impractical continues today. Is this criticism a myth or reality? How relevant is teacher education today?

The teachers surveyed generally believed that their own pre-service teacher education experience was quite relevant to their practice. Nine out of ten teachers (87 percent) found their pre-service teacher education to be somewhat (34 percent), mostly (42 percent), or very (11 percent) relevant. Although this provides some positive feedback to dispel the myth of the ivory tower, it still leaves a substantial number of teachers who described their pre-service teacher education experience as mostly (12 percent) or very (1 percent) irrelevant.

One high school social studies teacher believed that teacher education needed to address "real" teaching rather than "ideal" teaching. A middle school science teacher reported that "the two blocks of classes [in education] were mostly about theory and abstract topics. They did not prepare me for the day-to-day life [of] a teacher." As you meet some of the teachers later in this book, the issue of relevance will come up again and again.

Interestingly, the viewpoints expressed by the teachers again varied significantly by gender. Female teachers (with a mean score of 3.64 on a five point scale) rated their pre-service teacher education experience as more relevant than their male counterparts (with a mean score of 3.28 on a five point scale). This result was statistically significant ($t(187) = -2.80$, $p < 0.01$).

The relevance of pre-service teacher education reported by the teachers also varied significantly by subject area. Teachers of technology education (with an average score of 3.89), music (with an average score of 3.80), and foreign languages (with an average score of 3.77) rated the relevance of pre-service teacher education significantly higher ($F(8, 178) = 2.21$, $p < 0.05$).

Conversely, teachers of science (with an average score of 3.40), math (with an average score of 3.20), and social studies (with an average score of 3.20) rated the relevance of pre-service teacher education significantly lower. It is particularly interesting to note that the teachers in the core subject areas found their pre-service teacher education experiences to be less relevant than those in several elective areas.

INFLUENCE

As we just learned, roughly nine out of ten teachers found their own pre-service teacher education experience to be somewhat, mostly, or very relevant. Based on this result, one might expect that pre-service teacher education had a large influence on how they teach. In particular, one might expect a methods course, where students learn about teaching methods, to be especially influential. A teaching methods course is a standard component in most pre-service teacher education programs. What is the influence of the pre-service methods course on teachers? What is the influence of the pre-service teacher education program in general? Do teachers generally feel well prepared to teach?

The influence of the methods course on teachers was considerable. Four out of five teachers reported using some (49 percent), a lot (30 percent), or all (2 percent) of the teaching methods learned in their university methods course during their student teaching. While the majority of teachers did use what was taught in the university methods course, there were teachers who reported using little (17 percent) to none (2 percent) of the teaching methods they were taught. As a teacher educator, and someone who has taught a methods course, I have to admit that I was more than a little disappointed in this result. Once again, gender was a large factor (t(187) = −2.326, p < 0.05). Female teachers (with an average score of 3.24 on a five point scale) reported using the strategies taught in methods more frequently during student teaching than their male counterparts (with an average score of 2.97 on a five point scale).

The teachers were also asked how much they use the methods they learned in the university methods course in their current teaching. As might be expected, the teaching methods used by teachers do change over the course of one's teaching career. Even so, three out of five teachers reported still using some (42 percent) or a lot (17 percent) of the teaching methods learned in their university methods course during their current teaching. The remaining teachers reported using little (32 percent) to none (9 percent). As in the previous question, the most frequent response was that teachers use "some" of the teaching methods they learned in the university methods course.

As expected, it was found that the amount of influence of the methods course decreased from student teaching (with an average score of 3.13) to current teaching (with an average score of 2.69). As teachers continue to learn and implement new strategies for teaching and learning through professional development, new methods may replace old methods. However, if teachers continue to learn new teaching strategies throughout their careers, one might expect that the teaching methods of younger teachers would more closely reflect what was taught in their methods course as compared to that of older teachers. Based upon the results of the survey, this was not the case.

There was not a statistically significant difference in the response to this question based upon either age or years of experience. This suggested that the teaching methods from the methods courses are either retained or discarded very early, likely within the first few years of teaching. Although there was not a significant difference based on age, there was a statistically significant difference based on gender ($t(184) = -2.43$, $p < 0.05$) with females (with an average score of 2.82 on a five point scale) reporting using the methods from their methods course in their current teaching more than males (with an average score of 2.51 on a five point scale).

The methods course does have an influence on how teachers are teaching their classes during their student teaching and throughout their teaching careers. How effective is pre-service teacher education in general? Do teachers generally feel well prepared for teaching? The vast majority of teachers do. Nine out of ten teachers (85 percent) reported feeling somewhat (39 percent), mostly (34 percent), or very (12 percent) prepared for their first year of teaching. Relatively few teachers felt mostly (13 percent) or very (2 percent) unprepared to begin their teaching careers.

However, one must also consider that those teachers who felt the least prepared in their first year of teaching may have left the profession in their first five years. Research shows that nearly half of teachers leave the profession by the end of their fifth year (Gold, 1996; Haberman, 1996; National Commission, 1996). The views of those teachers are obviously not represented in a survey of teachers.

GAPS IN PREPARATION

Despite the generally positive feedback from teachers about the effectiveness and influence of pre-service teacher education, the teachers surveyed did identify several gaps in their own pre-service preparation. In particular, the teachers identified a number of issues and challenges for which their pre-service teacher education did not prepare them. There were a total of 302 comments from 163 teachers (85 percent) when asked, "What, if anything, were you not prepared for in your first year?"

By far, the most common issue teachers felt unprepared for in their first year of teaching was the issue of classroom management. In fact, seventy-nine of the teachers surveyed (41 percent) said they were not prepared for issues related to classroom management. These included the issues of student behavior, difficult students, discipline, classroom management problems, and classroom management strategies. One high school chemistry and physics teacher declared that "discipline is the most difficult part when you begin teaching."

Many other teachers agreed. A high school Spanish teacher explained that he was simply not prepared for "how to deal with discipline problems and students from dysfunctional households." A middle school English and social studies teacher described what she learned in her classroom management course as merely "cute ideas." In contrast, another high school Spanish teacher remarked that he needed "actual practice and tips" to be better prepared for classroom management as a first year teacher. This topic seemed to underscore the difficulty that some teachers had in connecting theory to practice in their pre-service teacher education experience.

Classroom management was, by far, the issue that the most teachers identified in the survey, but it wasn't the only thing they felt unprepared to handle. One in five teachers (20 percent) reported feeling unprepared for the workload and amount of paperwork in their first year of teaching. One high school geometry teacher stated, "I was overwhelmed by the amount of preparing you must do and the amount of paperwork." A middle school art teacher mentioned "all the meetings we must attend, all the paperwork we have, like grades, reports to parents, IEP forms." Other teachers talked about the number of classes, forms, "office business," and the "busy work associated with teaching."

According to one Spanish teacher, one of the things that made managing paperwork difficult for new teachers was "having to 'teach' at the same time." In this respect, managing the workload and amount of paperwork of a teacher was compounded by the limited time available during the school day to complete these tasks. Related to the workload, 14 percent of teachers reported feeling unprepared to manage their time, which is essential for any teacher and often difficult for new teachers. The teachers identified the "lack of prep time," the "extra duties," and "the amount of time that planning, grading, and administrative tasks took" as considerable challenges for new teachers.

For these teachers, pre-service teacher education did not help them to develop the knowledge and skills they needed to efficiently organize and manage their time and classroom responsibilities. In many respects, these issues relate back to the need for more practical preparation in the area of classroom management. More specifically, it calls attention to the need for classroom management in pre-service teacher education that includes, but is not limited to student behavior and discipline. Pre-service teacher education must also address the knowledge and skills teachers use to manage time, paperwork, files, grading, policies, procedures, communications, facilities, equipment, supplies, and safety concerns.

Many teachers (16 percent) also identified working with parents and families as a challenge of teaching for which they felt unprepared. One high school mathematics teacher stated quite frankly, "I was not prepared when it came to dealing with parents." A high school Spanish teacher said they didn't know what to do "when they [parents] go nuts on you." Another high school mathematics teacher was surprised at the "amount of social work not math needed to help students become successful." As you can imagine, this teacher had to adapt their views on the role of the teacher, when faced with the realities of working with students and families.

The pressures faced by teachers are not just from students and families. Some of the challenges come from within the school: 13 percent of teachers reported feeling unprepared for dealing with administration and the politics of schools. Pre-service teachers were often unaware and uneducated about the politics that may exist in a school building or district. The teachers specifically mentioned feeling unprepared to understand issues related to school contracts, unions, benefits, politics, cynical colleagues, and financial issues.

Although teaching methods are typically taught in pre-service teacher education, some teachers (10 percent) did not feel prepared for some of the more practical issues related to planning and teaching lessons. For example, one high school chemistry teacher was not prepared for "how to prepare labs" as a first year teacher. Another high school science teacher mentioned that they were not prepared for "having to work around supplies and equipment that were available" when designing lessons. Finally, several teachers alluded to the need for more practical teaching strategies to be taught in pre-service teacher education, in contrast to the "theory and abstract topics" or "ideal teaching" presented in their teaching methods courses.

Curriculum is another topic that is often thoroughly addressed in the education courses for pre-service teachers. Nonetheless, 8 percent of teachers reported feeling unprepared to deal with the curriculum of the courses they teach. One high school business teacher commented that new teachers should be prepared for "the possibility of finding a poor or non-existent curriculum and [the] need to create as you go forward." A high school English teacher felt that she had not learned the "actual content that a middle school student learns" during her university pre-service teacher education coursework.

A portion of teachers (6 percent) also reported feeling unprepared to assess student learning. One high school technology education teacher felt unprepared for "various grading/assessment methods" needed to assess student learning. A high school social studies teacher reported feeling unprepared specifically for "test writing." In another case, a high school English teacher was unprepared to develop assessments for "ESL students," students with English as a second language.

Finally, a portion of teachers (5 percent) also reported feeling unprepared for planning lessons. In particular, one high school social studies teacher reported feeling unprepared to plan lessons "at an appropriate level the students could understand." Another high school mathematics teacher commented that her student teaching experience was not very helpful in preparing her to plan lessons. She stated, "In student-teaching I mostly used the materials already prepared by my coop. teacher. I had no idea how to prep. for an entire year of material by myself."

Finally, a middle and high school French teacher complained that the lesson plans created in her pre-service teacher education courses were "really ideal lessons." She found these types of lessons "impossible" to create "with all the other responsibilities a teacher has." According to this teacher, "That disconnect can be painful and damaging to one's sense of professional efficacy." In other words, the expectations for planning lessons were set so high that new teachers are unable to plan lessons in the same way in their first year of teaching. As a result, they face a sense of failure when they begin teaching.

By identifying what teachers felt unprepared to address as first year teachers, these teachers identified a variety of gaps in pre-service teacher preparation. Figure 4.1 provides a graph of these gaps in preparation along with the percentage of teachers reporting feeling unprepared for each one. This list of topics that teachers reported feeling unprepared to address in their first year of teaching provides teacher educators valuable feedback for improving pre-service teacher education. It is ultimately the responsibility of teacher educators to design classroom and field experiences for pre-service teachers that address these issues.

Interestingly, the top five issues for which teachers felt unprepared—classroom management, workload and paperwork, time management, parents, and administration and politics—may arguably be issues that are best addressed in the context of meaningful field experiences. This only reinforces the need for strong partnerships between schools and universities in preparing future teachers. While many pre-service teacher education programs are now engaged in professional development school partnerships with K–12 schools, the extent to which these practical issues of teaching and schools are being leveraged to prepare pre-service teachers for these issues is still often inadequate.

The remaining issues identified by teachers—teaching methods, curriculum, assessment, and planning lessons—are typically addressed quite thoroughly in the university-based pre-service teacher education courses.

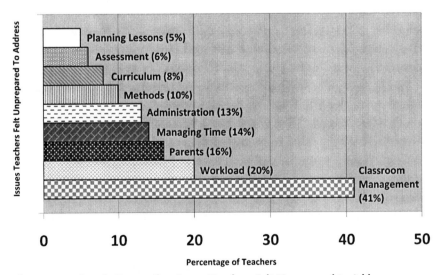

Figure 4.1.   Gaps in Preparation: Issues Teachers Felt Unprepared to Address

Nonetheless, the comments and feedback from teachers indicate that there is room for improvement. Some of the teachers used the words ideal, abstract, and theoretical to describe their pre-service teacher education courses. Based on these comments, one can conclude that pre-service teachers need help drawing connections between theory and practice. Like all students, they need experiences that prepare them to apply what they are learning in these courses in a real classroom with real students.

5

What Teachers Really Think
about Current Teacher Education

In addition to finding out what teachers think about their own pre-service teacher education experience, the survey asked teachers about current teacher education. This section of the survey asked practicing teachers questions about the current state of pre-service teacher education. The complete survey results can be seen in appendix C. In the survey responses, the teachers expressed their satisfactions, concerns, and opinions on the current state of pre-service teacher education. They also provided their opinion on current issues such as standards-based teacher education, professional development school partnerships, and alternative certification programs for teacher licensure.

As mentioned earlier, there has been a great deal of research done on pre-service teacher education. However, the vast majority of the research on teacher education involves the study of pre-service teachers. The views and performance of pre-service teachers can be studied in a wide variety of ways. They are also a readily available group of participants to most teacher educators, who are often attempting to study the effectiveness or effect of their own practices. Pre-service teachers can evaluate and reflect on their experiences immediately after completing a course, field experience, or program. Their performance during student teaching or during their first few years of teaching can also be studied, which reflects on their preparation in the program.

Although this type of research is common in teacher education, there are two significant limitations. First, the researcher is typically studying their own pre-service teachers and evaluating the effectiveness of their own practices. This presents an obvious bias for the researcher. Second, this limits the evaluation of pre-service teacher education to its immediate effect on pre-service teachers. As a profession that highly values lifelong learning, the lack of attention to the long term effects of teacher education on teachers is somewhat ironic. The unfortunate truth is that very few studies in teacher education involve in-service teachers beyond their first few years of teaching.

The teachers in this study had the advantages of experience (seventeen years of experience on average) and hindsight in reflecting on pre-service teacher education. These teachers have had time to reflect on teaching and teacher education. Although the teachers surveyed are not experts in teacher education, they are experienced in the art and science of teaching. They understand the needs of the practitioner in today's schools. For this reason, these teachers can provide valuable insights to complement the expert views of teacher educators or the knowledge gained from the study of pre-service teachers. What do these teachers think of current pre-service teacher education programs? Some of their views may surprise you.

SATISFACTION

According to the survey, slightly less than half of teachers are mostly (42 percent) or very (4 percent) satisfied with the current state of teacher education. By comparison, one out of four teachers were mostly (22 percent) or very (3 percent) unsatisfied. Although one could argue that there is more satisfaction than dissatisfaction among teachers, the number of teachers who are unsatisfied with current pre-service teacher education should be quite distressing to teacher educators.

The fact that the remaining 29 percent expressed "no opinion" should also be concerning. It could be that this 29 percent have not paid attention or been involved in pre-service teacher education, since they received their pre-service education. Even worse, these teachers may have little concern for how new teachers are prepared for the profession. Given how teachers are routinely disrespected and scapegoated by students, parents, community members, and the media, these teachers may have simply lost hope or interest in the future of their own profession.

In general, teachers were slightly more pleased with their own pre-service teacher education experience (with an average score of 3.39 on a five point scale) than current pre-service teacher education (with an average rating of 3.23 on a five point scale). This could be a reflection of the negativity about teachers and teacher education that has been growing for the past thirty years. Since *A Nation at Risk* (NCEE, 1983) was published, the field of education has been heavily criticized by the public, and especially by lawmakers.

Sadly, even educators have turned on one another. Researchers and teacher educators routinely condemn the current state of K–12 schools and school teachers in their writing. At the same time, teachers criticize teacher educators for their ivory tower perspective on teaching and learning.

Perhaps even educators are beginning to believe in the ineptitude of their own profession. If so, the attitudes and cultures conveyed in schools and universities may need to be transformed. Although many will not agree, the accountability movement that teachers love to hate may provide the evidence we need to stand up for the effectiveness of teachers and teacher educators.

One interesting similarity between the teachers' views of their own pre-service teacher education experience and current pre-service teacher education is the role that gender played in the responses. Once again, female teachers (with an average score of 3.57 on a five point scale) assessed current pre-service teacher education more favorably than male teachers (with an average score of 3.04 on a five point scale).

Although the difference may appear small, the statistical analysis shows that this difference based on gender is statistically significant ($t(180) = -2.37$, $p < 0.05$). Because of the lack of research in this area, this raises more questions than answers. It also highlights the need for further study of gender in teacher preparation and the need for the recruitment and retention of men in education.

REASONS FOR DISSATISFACTION

The teachers who were dissatisfied with current pre-service teacher education expressed multiple reasons for their dissatisfaction. There were a total of 129 comments given by 100 different teachers to explain their satisfaction or dissatisfaction with the current state of pre-service teacher education. These comments reveal what teachers liked and disliked about current teacher preparation programs.

Overall, the comments focused almost entirely on the negative, or the reasons for their dissatisfaction with current pre-service teacher education. Of the 129 comments, only 25 were positive comments explaining why teachers were satisfied. Teachers praised teacher education for earlier field experiences, developing content knowledge, and teaching cooperative learning strategies. Nonetheless, the positive comments were the exception. There were many more negative comments than positive ones.

There were six main reasons for teachers' dissatisfactions with preservice teacher education that emerged from the teachers' responses to this open-ended survey question. The five reasons included: a lack of practical preparation, bad experiences with student teachers, shortages or shortcomings of field experiences, poor preparation in classroom management, and the hoops required for initial certification. The remaining comments were placed into a category for other reasons. The reasons for teachers' dissatisfactions can be seen in figure 5.1, along with the number of comments from teachers in each category.

The most common dissatisfaction expressed by teachers was the lack of practical preparation. This is consistent with the perceived theory-practice

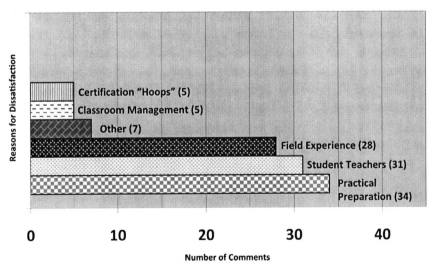

Figure 5.1.   Reasons for Dissatisfaction with Pre-Service Teacher Education

gap between what is taught in teacher education and what is practiced in the classroom, which will be discussed later in this chapter. It is also consistent with the "ivory tower" criticism often bestowed upon pre-service teacher education (Book, 1996, p. 207). More specifically, this theme included suggestions from teachers for more practical instructional methods, more emphasis on application, less busy work, and more emphasis on professionalism and other responsibilities.

One sixth grade teacher commented that current pre-service teacher education seems to be "a great deal of fluff and busy work." This dissatisfaction with pre-service teacher education is a direct attack on the rigor of teacher education curriculum and assignments. A high school mathematics and social studies teacher attacked teacher educators by saying that "professors had no touch with the real teaching world." Although this may be true of some professors of education, it certainly cannot be true of all.

The professional development school model, which will be discussed in the next chapter, is one reform aimed at addressing this criticism. This also raises the question of how much teachers are willing to become involved in pre-service teacher education. If teachers are not willing to partner with teacher educators, then the complaints about out of touch teacher educators is just noise. If teachers are to be connected with practitioners, partnerships must be carefully established and maintained.

Another high school social studies teacher lamented the idealism of current pre-service teacher education.

> The idealism found in schools of ed is unrealistic. Students are taught that high schoolers love to be there and are itching to learn. . . . It is also unrealistic for colleges to teach students that every lesson must be perfect—there is no perfect lesson. I was made to feel a failure if every day was not scintillating and cutting edge. It's just not realistic.

For one elementary and middle school music teacher, the need for more practical preparation for pre-service teachers was not about what was taught or how it was taught. Rather, it was about what was not taught. This teacher was dissatisfied with current pre-service teacher education because it did not prepare new teachers for "the day to day classroom behavioral issues, budget and supplies, [and] identification of special needs students."

This teacher believed that pre-service teachers enter the classroom with "adequate basic skills." The term adequate is not exactly a glowing endorsement, but it sounds slightly better than unrealistic. Of course, when a teacher cannot adequately manage classroom behavior or resources, even the perfect lesson plan would be inadequate. The ability to teach students with special needs, which was identified above, is equally essential. Preparing teachers to teach in a classroom where every student responds equally well to the same instruction really is unrealistic.

Every student, even those without an individualized education plan (IEP), has special needs; teachers must plan their lessons to meet the needs of all learners. This is certainly an area for improvement in pre-service teacher education. A middle school English teacher commented, "It seems that nobody's child is average anymore." She emphasized that teachers "need to be ready for the challenges of special ed and gifted/talented students."

Pre-service teachers must be better prepared with practical strategies to develop a more student-centered approach to curriculum, instruction, and assessment. Although strategies for the inclusion of students with special needs is currently taught in pre-service teacher education, it would seem that it all still seems impractical to most teachers, pre-service or inservice. A high school geometry teacher insisted, "Teachers need more preparation on how to deal with students who have learning disabilities or other disabilities." This is one aspect of providing more practical preparation for pre-service teachers.

The second most common reason that teachers are dissatisfied with current teacher education is the product they are producing, namely student teachers. Practicing teachers are not happy with the quality of the student teachers that are being produced by current pre-service teacher education programs. They are unhappy with the professionalism of student teachers. More specifically, they identified the poor motivation, attitude, and commitment of student teachers as some of their most serious concerns. For these teachers, the poor quality of the student teachers or recent graduates they observed reflected very poorly on the pre-service teacher education program as a whole.

These comments from teachers provided some evidence that the teachers surveyed may have used their experiences with student teachers as a basis for assessing current pre-service teacher education. It is certainly true in regards to their dissatisfactions with pre-service teacher education and may be true of their responses to other questions as well. In this regard, it may be that teachers were more aware or attentive to the final product of pre-service teacher education, beginning teachers, than the curriculum, instruction, or assessment involved in the process of teacher preparation. Some teachers, especially recent graduates, also made reference to their own teacher education experiences when commenting on current pre-service teacher education.

One high school science teacher who had worked with several student teachers commented that the student teachers "seemed to know their stuff." I can only assume this was a reference to the student teachers' knowledge of content and pedagogy. The teacher continued, "All of them, however, were not prepared for all of the work and time commitments teaching requires." Another high school mathematics teacher said, "I am not directly involved with these candidates and do NOT feel comfortable with the attitude of recent candidates."

Yet another high school mathematics teacher described his most recent student teacher as "ill prepared and unmotivated." Interestingly, he also had another recent student teacher who was "outstanding and highly motivated." Both of the student teachers came from the same pre-service teacher education program. In this case, it may not be the effectiveness of the program, but the rigor and selectivity of the program that is the source of dissatisfaction.

In listening to these criticisms, one could argue that this is simply an extension of the natural phenomena where each generation complains about the following generation. The baby boomers were selfish, Generation X was lazy, and the Millenials have been affectionately called the boomerang generation, for their renowned ability to return home to live with their parents after college. This may be one of the reasons that teachers are dissatisfied with current pre-service teacher education. On the other hand, it could be more than your typical contempt for a younger generation.

The criticisms from teachers about the quality of student teachers could also reflect negatively on the quality of students admitted to university schools of education. Some have argued that university teacher education programs must be more selective in admitting students as education majors. Unlike many of the highest performing countries on standardized exams (such as Finland, Singapore, or South Korea), teachers in the United States are not typically selected from the top tier of university students.

Sadly, the academic qualifications of education majors have lagged behind other college majors for some time. In 2011, for example, those students intending to major in education scored an average composite score of 20.6 on the ACT, slightly below the average composite score of 21.1 (ACT, 2011). The students who intended to major in education scored considerably lower than those with intended majors in mathematics or computer science (22.1), science (23.8), or English or foreign language (23.9) (ACT, 2011). On a list of college majors, the average composite score of education majors was ranked fourteen out of the eighteen intended majors listed (ACT, 2011).

Raising the admissions criteria of university teacher education programs could successfully improve the quality of student teachers and teachers. In order to be selective, however, there must be a large pool of candidates who are interested in becoming teachers. The reality is that fewer university students are interested in education today, and schools of education have suffered drastically declining enrollments over the past forty years.

During the 1970–1971 academic year, there were 176,307 graduates who earned a bachelor's degree in education (NCES, 2011). During the 2009–2010 academic year, there were 101,265 graduates who earned a bachelor's degree in education (NCES, 2011). The enrollments are often dangerously low, especially in subject areas like science, technology, engineering, and mathematics (STEM).

How can university teacher education programs be more selective at a time when the pool of candidates is so small? For these programs, raising the admissions requirements for schools of education would seem unthinkable, even suicidal for some programs. If the profession is not made more attractive to talented candidates, then added selectivity in admissions is just not feasible. The resulting low enrollments would only add to the growing teacher shortages in many parts of the United States.

In order to raise the selectivity and admissions requirements in teacher education programs, we must also raise the status and attractiveness of the teaching profession, especially in high need subject areas like science, technology, engineering, mathematics, and special education. This could include improvements in salary compensation, benefits, workloads, working conditions, or opportunities for advancement. It may also involve a publicity campaign to recognize and value teachers as important contributors to schools and society, not the saviors or scapegoats of the educational system.

It is also important to recognize that some highly valued qualities of pre-service teachers are not related to their academic qualifications. You may have noticed that many of the qualities that teachers bemoaned were dispositional issues, such as attitude, motivation, and commitment. While professionalism is something that is highly valued, it is difficult to measure or teach. Nonetheless, it requires the attention of teacher educators. This is where the accountability measures in teacher education fall short. They ignore the human qualities that make an excellent student an excellent teacher. As is evident in the teachers' comments, these qualities cannot be ignored in teacher education.

Field experience was another common theme among the comments received from teachers. These comments included dissatisfaction with the amount and requirements of field experiences. One high school Spanish teacher concluded that pre-service teachers simply "need more time in the classroom." If the job of a teacher is to facilitate the social, emotional, and intellectual growth of children, then pre-service teachers need more time and experiences with kids. These are not skills that university students can develop in a university classroom.

It also included some specific complaints or suggestions from those who had worked as cooperating teachers. One middle school art teacher was dissatisfied with the requirements placed on the student teacher during student teaching. She commented that the university "expects too much paperwork from student teachers." In her opinion, "They are overwhelmed."

A middle and high school French teacher criticized the field experience for not requiring the pre-service teachers to be more engaged in the classroom during pre-student teaching field experiences. This teacher commented, "Practicum programs are too passive." She added, "I think it's important for pre-service teachers to see and participate in some of the 'non-educational' tasks that teacher must do (e.g., committee work, building/district initiatives, etc.)."

Although most of the comments were negative, one high school English teacher did express her satisfaction with the field experience component in her local pre-service teacher education program. She said, "Seems like teachers these days, in this area, are in the classroom sooner and for longer times and I think this sort of hands-on experience is the most beneficial."

In her opinion, increasing the amount of time that pre-service teachers spend engaged in field experiences was one of the things that current teacher education is doing well. The value of earlier and extended field experiences for pre-service teachers is also well supported in the research literature (Darling-Hammond, Wise, & Klein, 1995; Ewing & Smith, 2002; Huling, 1998; Martin, Munby, & Hutchinson, 1998; Upitis, 1999).

Another reason for teachers' dissatisfaction with pre-service teacher education was the lack of preparation in classroom management. If you remember, classroom management was also identified in the last chapter as an area for which many teachers felt unprepared. One middle school mathematics teacher argued that pre-service teachers did "not [have] enough discipline experiences." Another middle and high school English teacher added that "most student teachers in our building seem prepared for content, but seem to lack discipline/management skills."

It is noteworthy that the teachers use the terms experience and skills, rather than coursework or knowledge. Adding another course in classroom management may not sufficiently address this issue. Rather, to gain experience and skill, a pre-service teacher may benefit more from a well-structured practicum or pre-student teaching experiences. In the field, the pre-service teacher can practice the skills required to manage the lesson, the classroom environment, and student behavior in an authentic context.

The final reason for dissatisfaction with current pre-service teacher education was the number of requirements, or hoops as they are sometimes called, for initial certification. These could include university or state requirements, as the teachers did not really distinguish between the two. One middle school art teacher remarked that "too much is required of new teachers. There are too many hoops to go through."

His concern was that these requirements are deterring talented and qualified individuals from entering the teaching profession. He rhetorically asked, "Who's going to want to teach!!??" Even if you are not a fan of the multiple punctuation marks at the end of his comment, his point is well taken. Some in the field of education would agree and continue to push for deregulation of the teaching profession, leaving more local control to school districts and universities.

Conversely, one physical education teacher did note that teacher education has "made teachers become more accountable in the way they get certified." Whether this teacher intended this as a compliment or criticism is unknown. What is known is that teachers have noticed the increased requirements for entering the profession. One middle school art teacher praised current teacher education for the use of "portfolios and cross-curricular lesson planning." According to this teacher, "They [pre-service teacher education] seemed to have improved since I was in college."

THEORY-PRACTICE GAP

In the field of education, there is often a widely perpetuated stereotype that teacher education is overly theoretical. At times, teachers disparage the value of educational research, pre-service teacher education, and in-service teacher education as missing an element of pragmatism. If the theoretical framework and concepts conveyed in research or teacher education seem impractical, it is labeled as "theory," as if it were a four letter word.

The term theory is seldomly used positively to convey a well-researched or evidence-based explanation, with good reliability, validity, and generalizability. As a result, the difference between what is taught in pre-service teacher education and what is practiced in the classroom is often referred to as a theory-practice gap. Is the gap between theory and practice a myth or a reality?

According to the teachers surveyed, it is a reality. The dissatisfaction with pre-service teacher education and the expressed need for more practical preparation is evidence of teachers' concerns about the theory-practice gap. When talking to the more jaded teachers among us, this gap is enormous and insurmountable. How many teachers believe there is a significant gap between how teachers are taught to teach and how they actually teach? This question was posed to teachers.

Nearly half of practicing teachers (45 percent) believed there was a significant (42 percent) or very significant gap (3 percent) between what is taught and what is practiced in K–12 classrooms. By comparison, one in five teachers (22 percent) believed there was an insignificant gap (21 percent) and only 1 percent said there was no gap at all. One-third of teachers surveyed (33 percent) responded no opinion to this question. Some teachers may not have been familiar enough with current pre-service teacher education programs or what is taught in a methods course to answer the question.

According to teachers, there is a theory-practice gap in the field of education, a gap between what is discussed in teacher preparation programs and what is practiced in the field. This commonly held belief may help to explain some of the dissatisfaction with current pre-service teacher education. It may also present a goal and an opportunity for improvement for both teachers and teacher educators. Teachers need support to better understand and utilize educational theories to inform their practice. Teacher educators need support to make better and more explicit connections between theory and practice.

PROFESSIONAL DEVELOPMENT SCHOOLS

One of the dissatisfactions with current pre-service teacher education expressed by some of the teachers was education professors, or teacher educators, who are out of touch. If the teacher educators are out of touch, the preparation of pre-service teachers would most certainly be inadequate. As we just learned, nearly half of teachers believed there was a significant (42 percent) or very significant gap (3 percent) between what is taught in pre-service teacher education and the realities of teaching in today's schools. Earlier in the book, some teachers went so far as to describe their experience in pre-service teacher education as mostly (12 percent) or very (1 percent) irrelevant.

One approach to connecting theory and practice and making teacher preparation more relevant is developing partnerships between schools and universities. One model for establishing and maintaining these partnerships is the professional development school. A professional development school is an elementary, middle, or high school that partners with a university education program in order to improve student achievement and pre-service teacher education (Teitel, 2003). In the *Handbook of Research on Teacher Education*, Boyle-Baise and McIntyre stated that "authentic collaboration and partnership between institutions of higher education and P–12 schools are at the core of the PDS concept" (2008, p. 317).

In this partnership, teachers and teacher educators work together in achieving the goals of both the school, to educate students, and the university, to prepare and educate teachers for effective careers in teaching (Teitel, 2003). The teachers of professional development schools often become more involved in the process of pre-service teacher education and occasionally more involved in educational research (Boyle-Baise & McIntyre, 2008).

At the same time, university teacher educators become more involved in the continuing education and professional development of teachers and maintain a better awareness of the environment of K–12 classrooms (Teitel, 2003). According to Boyle-Baise and McIntyre, "PDS advocates believe that schooling and teacher education are intertwined and that transformative change of either endeavor cannot occur without collaboration between the two partners" (2008, p. 317).

The idea for having schools with close working relationships with university pre-service teacher education programs first emerged in the early twentieth century. At that time, John Dewey, a famous and influential American educator, expressed a desire for what he then called "laboratory schools" (Hallinan & Khmelkov, 2001, p. 180). In the 1960s and 1970s, "portal schools" operated in a limited role in pre-service teacher education in the United States (Stallings & Kowalski, 1990).

The idea reemerged in the literature on multiple occasions over the next several decades. The names partner schools, clinical schools, teaching schools, professional practice schools, and professional development academies were all used at one time or another to describe what is now most commonly known as a professional development school. Although the concept of professional development schools has existed for many years, the use of professional development schools as a reform strategy received much more praise, consideration, and implementation in the 1990s.

The current conceptualization of professional development schools found in literature and in practice is an amalgamation and revision of these predecessors. The considerable work of many individual researchers, the RAND Corporation (Wise & Darling-Hammond, 1987), the Holmes Group (1990, 1995), and the National Commission on Teaching and America's Future (1996) have also added much to the present state of professional development schools. None was more influential in shaping and promoting the use of professional development schools than the Holmes Group.

In 1990, the Holmes Group released a report entitled *Tomorrow's Schools: Principles for the Design of Professional Development Schools.* In it they made a persuasive argument that professional development schools were a necessary strategy for the successful reform and improvement of pre-service teacher education. The authors laid out a framework of ideas about what professional development schools should be like, how they should be formed, and how they should operate. Many of those recommendations have had a lasting influence on the professional development schools in operation today.

In 1995, the Holmes Group published another report entitled *Tomorrow's Schools of Education.* In this report, the Holmes Group confronted and admonished pre-service teacher education programs of the 1980s for failing to develop meaningful partnerships with elementary, middle, and high schools (1995). Their accusations supported the common notion among many teachers, that teacher education was aloof and out of touch (Book, 1996).

Soon after the second Holmes Group report, the National Commission on Teaching and America's Future published a report entitled *What Matters Most: Teaching for America's Future* (1996). This report extensively commented on the state of education in the United States and made recommendations for future reforms. The report compared the U.S. system of education to other industrialized nations and found the United States was failing in comparison.

Nations of similar economic status employed more teachers, paid them a higher salary, provided them more time for preparation and collaboration, and gave them more responsibility and authority in making decisions regarding education (National Commission on Teaching and America's Future, 1996). These findings confirmed the need for teachers to play a broader and more significant role in the field of education. This report also provided support for the professional development school reform, which provided opportunities to connect teachers with teacher educators.

A variety of research has demonstrated the positive effects and characteristics of professional development schools on teacher education (Abdal-Haqq, 1998; Darling-Hammond, 1994a; Hallinan & Khmelkov, 2001; Petrie, 1995; Valli, Cooper, & Frankes, 1997). Studies have shown that pre-service teachers prepared in a PDS setting were more effective in managing student behavior, generating student interest in learning, and providing timely feedback (Houston et al., 1999; Share et al., 1999; Stallings, 1991; Wait, 2000). A study in the state of Texas found that the attrition rate for new teachers who had been trained in professional development schools was one-third of the rate of new teachers from traditional teacher education programs (Fleener, 1999).

So what do teachers think about professional development schools? Are they willing to form these types of partnerships with local university teacher education programs? The answer is yes. In fact, two-thirds of teachers (66 percent) indicated they would probably (50 percent) or definitely (16 percent) be in favor of their school becoming a professional development school. A high school foreign language teacher remarked, "I would like to . . . I'm very proud of my school and I think the teachers have so much to give."

Another teacher said, "It is just the close proximity . . . we're just across town from it so I think that it would just be logical for us to be one, you know, and to share some of that information." This high school technology education teacher also mentioned that he would "like to be able to take my kids over to the university . . . to see some of the labs and use some of the labs." At the same time, he added, "I'd like to see them come over here and see our kids and work with our kids a little more because I think we're both going to benefit from it."

One high school social studies teacher supported partnerships between schools and university teacher preparation programs. He believed that the university faculty members could benefit the teachers and the students at his school. He suggested that the "professors could come here and say . . . we think this is good, but this needs to be tweaked a little, so that could work."

In particular, he believed that the university faculty members would bring a research perspective that may be missing and helpful to schools. He commented, "There's a lot of good research out there and if those professors could bring it in. . . .There's a lot of good stuff out there that nobody uses." He reported, "There are people in this building, to be honest, I don't think have ever read an educational journal since they graduated. . . .The professors tend to be a lot more research oriented."

Another high school social studies teacher believed that the student teachers could also benefit a professional development school. He explained, "I think the cooperating teacher, even like the department, can learn so much from a student teacher coming in with the latest, you know, knowing the latest research and learning styles, strategies, whatever it is." He believed having teachers, teacher educators, and student teachers all in the school and communicating with one another would produce "huge benefits." He added, "If all these people are there, they can all give that information, you can make better decisions for yourself; as a teacher I can make better decisions."

Most teachers agreed that professional development schools could be beneficial and were willing to form these types of partnerships with local universities. Only one in ten teachers (10 percent) said they would probably (9 percent) or definitely (1 percent) not want their school to become a professional development school. This showed promising support on the part of teachers to form professional development partnerships with university teacher education programs. This was true, even though most of the teachers (88 percent) did not teach in a professional development school.

Once again, the results also showed a statistically significant gender difference regarding both participation in professional development schools ($\chi^2(1, 186) = 5.31$, $p < .05$), and support for professional development schools ($t(144) = -3.06$, $p < .005$). Approximately one in six female teachers surveyed (16 percent) had taught in a professional development school compared to just one in twenty male teachers (5 percent).

In addition, female teachers showed significantly more support for professional development schools (with an average score of 3.87 on a five point scale) than their male counterparts (with an average score of 3.47 on a five point scale). It appears that women not only are more satisfied with pre-service teacher education, but are also more willing to establish a formal partnership with teacher educators.

STANDARDS

Like professional development schools, the standards reform in teacher education is a current reform strategy with a deep historical context. The implementation of standards, as well as the use of portfolios and other performance-based assessments, has had a significant influence on pre-service teacher education in the past twenty years. The standards in teacher education describe the knowledge, skills, and dispositions that students must possess to successfully complete the program and be licensed to teach by the state.

Pre-service teachers must demonstrate competency in each of these standards during their university coursework and field experiences. The use of a standards-based assessment system generally requires students to assemble a portfolio with artifacts and written reflections that demonstrate the students' competence on each standard. The standards-based reform of the 1990s had its historical roots in the 1920s.

One of the earliest forms of standards-based pre-service teacher education began as a result of the *Commonwealth Teacher Training Study* conducted by the University of Chicago between the years 1925 and 1928 (Charters & Waples, 1929). The study was an attempt to create and clarify the objectives and goals of university pre-service teacher education programs. It also attempted to incorporate scientific reasoning and empirical research methods to the decision-making process that would shape pre-service teacher education programs of that time.

In addition, it was thought that the development of standards might bring greater consistency to the variety of philosophies and methods used by pre-service teacher education programs across the United States (Charters & Waples, 1929). The *Commonwealth Teacher Training Study* gathered the ideas of educational professionals about the characteristics that defined quality teaching and quality teachers. The study sought input from parents, students, teachers, administrators, teacher unions, and teacher educators. The plethora of ideas was filtered by twenty-one judges who arrived at a list of eighty-three traits.

These traits were considered the benchmarks of effective teaching. Each trait had multiple indicators to determine if the students in a pre-service teacher education program were successfully demonstrating those traits. Charters and Waples surveyed practicing teachers and gathered a list of 1,001 activities that teachers commonly performed during teaching that would demonstrate the 83 traits previously identified (Charters & Waples, 1929). Clearly, the voice of teachers was well-represented during the development of the standards.

It was the intention of the researchers that the final list of 83 traits and 1,001 activities would be used by pre-service teacher education programs across the United States to reform the structures of their coursework and field experiences in order that students in education would successfully develop the necessary skills for effective teaching prior to entrance into the teaching profession. As it turns out, the standards developed by the *Commonwealth Teacher Training Study* had very little effect on pre-service teacher education programs of its time. The *Commonwealth Teacher Training Study* was significant because it introduced the United States to a standards-based approach to pre-service teacher education.

A number of other attempts at implementing standards into pre-service teacher education took place in the years that followed, with the same dismal results. In 1969, the standards reform in pre-service teacher education won a small victory when the U.S. Office of Education funded ten standards-based elementary teacher education programs at a cost of 1.3 million dollars (Clarke, 1969). The funding was accompanied by a national public relations campaign to promote the use of standards-based pre-service teacher education programs across the United States. It soon became a popular topic of discussion in educational journals and departments of education that lasted throughout the 1970s.

Like the earlier standards of the 1920s, the performance-based standards created during the 1970s were generally composed of a long list of desirable teacher characteristics and abilities. The standards produced by Michigan State University, for example, included 1,500 items that teachers should know or be able to do. Unlike the earlier standards, however, the performance-based standards of the 1970s were heavily laden with the language and ideas of behavioral psychology (McDonald, 1973).

Once again, the implementation of these ideas into the mainstream of pre-service teacher education was very limited. Only 13 percent of pre-service teacher education programs made a complete transition to a standards-based system of pre-service teacher education (Joyce, Howey, & Yarger, 1977; Sandefur & Nicklas, 1981). The vast majority continued the practice of using a course-based system where the completion of required courses determined the successful completion of a pre-service teacher education program.

There are many possible reasons for the failure of the early standards-based pre-service teacher education reforms to reach the mainstream of pre-service teacher education. One reason may have been the excessive length of the traits and activities. Incorporating such a long list of traits and activities into a typical pre-service teacher education program would have required a great deal of time and human resources that may not have been available for the typical underfunded and understaffed pre-service teacher education program. The assessment of standards would have simply added to the traditional assessment of coursework, not replaced it.

Second, the financial resources for designing standards and adapting the curriculum to implement those standards may not have been available to education departments. In the 1970s, it was estimated that the cost of developing a standards-based pre-service teacher education program was between 5 and 6 million dollars and the cost of running the program would be approximately 150 percent more than a traditional course-based program (Hite, 1973).

Finally, the use of performance-based standards necessarily placed a value on a defined set of characteristics or behaviors, while sometimes dismissing other potentially valuable or new aspects of teaching that are not included. In this way, the lists of traits and characteristics that were developed may have confined and restricted teacher educators. This is not a desirable effect. This remains a common criticism and legitimate concern for the use of standards and performance-based assessments in teacher education today.

The difficulties associated with implementing standards-based pre-service teacher education far outweighed the perceived benefits at that time and the push for standards would return to dormancy for another decade. In 1983, the report, *A Nation at Risk*, would change perceptions of education and satisfaction with pre-service teacher education in the United States. As mentioned previously, the report was highly critical of the methods and results of the American educational system. Particularly in the face of cold war competition and the expansion of a global economy, it was necessary for the United States to be competitive with other developed nations in economics, military, science, and technology.

Education was a primary means to increasing our global competitiveness and improving teacher quality was essential to improving our educational system. Therefore, pre-service teacher education was placed under the most intense scrutiny it had ever experienced and was challenged to find better ways of preparing teachers for successful and effective careers in the classroom. Under this new climate, the topic of standards-based pre-service teacher education made yet another comeback.

The return of standards-based pre-service teacher education to academic journals and the forefront of educational thought was a gradual process. It took time to find its way into legislation and state licensing requirements. The creation of the National Board for Professional Teaching Standards (NBPTS) and its standards for national board certification in 1987 was instrumental in leading the next generation of standards reform in teacher education.

Even though the National Board was funded and supported by federal and state governments, it was a private organization and not directly involved in the enterprise of pre-service teacher education. Nonetheless, it contributed to pre-service teacher education by developing a new set of standards for the teaching profession and reintroducing the concept of standards-based assessment. According to Linda Darling-Hammond, the NBPTS was used "to guide the work of the Interstate New Teacher Assessment and Support Consortium (INTASC)" (1999).

Subsequently, the National Council for Accreditation of Teacher Education (NCATE) incorporated the INTASC standards to assess and accredit university-based pre-service teacher education programs (Darling-Hammond, 1999). "While the standards each have a different function, i.e. teacher education accreditation (NCATE), initial licensing (INTASC), and advanced certification (NBPTS), they reinforce and complement each other through the kinds of criteria each requires in addressing the standards," according to Kraft (2001).

Many states relied heavily upon the professional standards developed by the NBPTS and INTASC to develop their own standards for teacher education and licensing. The ten Wisconsin teacher standards are nearly identical to the ten INTASC standards. The use of teacher standards has been widely adopted by the field of pre-service teacher education. According to Kraft, K–12 schools and pre-service teacher education programs have both "jumped on the standards 'bandwagon'" (2001, p. 1).

Today's teacher education standards are different from those of the 1970s. They are fewer in number and more general in nature than the list of hundreds or thousands of competencies that were common decades earlier. The standards today are also more reflective of the constructivist philosophies that now dominate pre-service teacher education, rather than the behaviorist philosophies that were more prevalent in the 1970s. The planning, revision, and implementation of standards reform in pre-service teacher education continues today at many universities around the nation. It has certainly been a catalyst for change for many pre-service teacher education programs.

Teachers were heavily involved in developing the National Board for Professional Teaching Standards (NBPTS) and the NBPTS was used to help develop the INTASC, NCATE, and many state teacher standards. However, the involvement of teachers in the latter stages of adapting and adopting the INTASC, NCATE, and most state teaching standards was considerably less. According to one group of educational researchers, "When practitioner input has been incorporated, it has frequently been in the form of teacher response to a list of competencies after they are adopted by an agency (professional, state, or local)" (Zionts, Shellady, & Zionts, 2006).

Another group of researchers even described their state's teacher standards as a "state-sanctioned view of learning as the mastery of discrete skills" (Kornfeld, Grady, Marker, & Ruddell, 2007). In this case, it was viewed as a top-down political reform, with little to no input from teachers or teacher educators. Education as a whole has experienced the control of state and federal legislators, and standards reform was no exception. There are many educational professionals who have contested that the field of education as a whole is "governed through lay political channels and government bureaucracies" (Darling-Hammond, Wise, & Klein, 1999, p. 5).

Shaker said, "In America the top policymakers for education are rarely educators or students of education" (2001, p. 2). Later in the same article, Shaker points out that "when they consult on educational matters, they are likely to listen to a combination of 'policy experts' (typically trained in variations of political science)" (2001, p. 3). Many question the ability of government to set the course for education reform and would rather see the involvement of teachers and other educators in the reform process.

Despite some criticism, the use of standards is now a widely accepted part of pre-service teacher education. Many teacher educators view standards-based pre-service teacher education as an effective approach to improving teacher quality and raising the status of the teaching profession by ensuring a higher standard of performance for state licensure. If done well, the use of standards in teacher education has the potential to create a more rigorous and focused curriculum. If not implemented carefully and thoughtfully, it may simply improve the ability of education students to create portfolios and strategically navigate the system.

So what do teachers think of the use of standards in pre-service teacher education? The results of the survey indicated strong support for a standards-based approach to pre-service teacher education. Seven out of ten teachers surveyed (72 percent) said they probably (53 percent) or definitely (19 percent) supported a standards-based approach. Once again, the support of a standards-based approach varied significantly by gender $(t(186) = -3.07, p < .005)$. The results showed that female teachers (with an average score of 3.93) supported a standards-based approach to pre-service teacher education significantly more than their male counterparts (with an average score of 3.50).

One of the reasons teachers were supportive of standards was that it provided a clear set of criteria that could be used to evaluate pre-service teachers throughout a program. The standards describe what a teacher should know or be able to do to be an effective teacher. Pre-service teachers can be evaluated based on these standards throughout their pre-service preparation; this ensures that each graduate has developed and demonstrated the necessary knowledge and skills in a variety of different ways. One high school foreign language teacher who had evaluated a student teacher using the state standards commented, "When I evaluated my student teacher, that [the standards] just gave me a good base for evaluation."

The use of portfolios to evaluate pre-service teachers is quite common in a standards-based approach to pre-service teacher education. According to the survey results, teachers were supportive of the use of portfolios in conjunction with course grades for the assessment of pre-service teachers. Three out of four teachers surveyed (74 percent) preferred that both course grades and portfolios be used to assess pre-service teachers. By comparison, one in eight teachers (12 percent) preferred that course grades be used alone and one in twenty-five (4 percent) preferred that portfolios be used alone.

While teachers were generally supportive of the use of standards and portfolio-based assessments in pre-service teacher education, some teachers expressed concern. A middle school science teacher commented that the standards are "pretty broad right now," which she felt made the assessment of pre-service teachers more difficult. The same teacher was also concerned that the state standards used to guide and measure pre-service teacher education had not been updated. She suggested, "If we're going to be doing that approach with pre-service teachers, make sure that [the standards] stays current."

One teacher believed that the attention to standards had taken away from focusing on the more intangible qualities, like professionalism and people skills. This high school technology education teacher said, "We're too much worried about meeting criteria and meeting standards." He said, "It all looks good on paper, but I don't know if it really means anything." He complained that pre-service teachers are not being prepared to "face kids in the classroom with the myriad of problems that they have."

Another teacher felt it led to far too much paperwork and other requirements and, in some cases, extended the time required to complete a degree in education. This teacher wrote:

> I am mostly concerned with the overwhelming requirements put up on students in education. The standards are too high. It takes many students five years now to complete the program with what benefits?

This high school mathematics teacher expressed a concern that many teacher educators have also expressed. The highly regulated system of initial certification of teachers may be driving some people away. As school budgets shrink and public criticisms of teachers grow, these barriers may outweigh the benefits, in the minds of some. This is a dangerous path to follow when certain subject areas (including special education, science, technology, and mathematics) and certain geographical areas (including the smallest rural districts, largest urban districts, and certain states) are already facing severe teacher shortages.

In many states, the teacher standards and portfolio-based assessments are also used as a requirement for the renewal of a teaching license. In Wisconsin, initial educators are required to complete a professional development plan (PDP) to demonstrate their growth on one or more of the state educator standards. One high school English teacher remarked, "As a PDP (PI 34) reviewer, I find new teachers bogged down in educational paperwork." She recommended "streamlining this requirement [for standards and portfolio-based assessments] so new teachers can concentrate on teaching." This appears to be the unintentional and unpopular side effect of a standards-based approach to teacher education and licensure.

ALTERNATIVE CERTIFICATION

While some have focused on improving traditional pre-service teacher education, others have worked to develop alternative pathways to certify teachers. For the most part, these alternative certification programs were initiated to address areas of teacher shortages. This includes geographical areas, such as the shortage of teachers in many urban areas. Other alternative certification programs are intended to meet shortages in specific subject areas, such as science, technology, mathematics, and special education.

Teacher shortages are nothing new to the educational community. Throughout the history of schooling in the United States, well-qualified teachers have been in short supply. The short supply of men willing to teach for the low salaries offered during the seventeenth and eighteenth centuries led to the inclusion of women in the teaching profession in the middle of the nineteenth century. During the eighteenth and nineteenth centuries, a well-qualified teacher might have been considered anyone who had completed the level of schooling they were entrusted to teach or, in some cases, one level higher. It wasn't until the twentieth century that most teachers were trained in a university pre-service teacher education program.

Today, educators, politicians, and the public believe that all teachers in public schools should be certified in the subjects they teach. Due to teacher shortages, this is not always the case. A significant number of teaching positions continue to be occupied by teachers who are not certified in the subjects they teach or not certified at all (Stoddart & Floden, 1989). This problem is particularly problematic in urban schools. The shortage of newly certified teachers graduating from university-based pre-service teacher education programs and entering urban schools has created pockets of drastic teacher shortage in the most urban areas of America.

Many qualified teachers choose not to teach in urban areas because of the challenging circumstances that exist in these schools and communities. According to studies, only 15 percent of education students say they would prefer to teach in urban areas (Zeichner & Hoeft, 1996). Instead, new teachers often compete for the more desired positions in suburban schools located in middle to upper class communities. Furthermore, many new teachers who begin their careers in urban schools will soon move to other schools when the opportunities arise or, in some cases, they will leave the teaching profession altogether.

The extent of teacher shortages also varies by subject area. Subjects such as science, mathematics, English as a second language (ESL), and special education are particularly short on certified teachers (Zeichner, 2003). Unfortunately, the burden of teacher shortages is usually faced by poorer states and poorer schools with fewer resources and a myriad of other challenges.

To make matters worse, the attrition rate in the teaching profession is much higher than most other professions and contributes significantly to teacher shortages in the United States. Approximately 15 percent of teachers in the United States leave after their first year, 25 percent leave by the end of the second year (Schlechty & Vance, 1983), and nearly half leave by the end of their fifth year (Gold, 1996; Haberman, 1996; National Commission on Teaching for America's Future, 1996).

Alternative certification attempts to supply teachers in shortage areas through nontraditional routes to certification. In their book *Alternative Routes to Teaching: Mapping the New Landscape of Teacher Education*, Grossman and Loeb defined alternative certification as "any pathway into teaching other than the traditional, college or university-based four-year teacher-preparation program" (2008, p. 4).

This definition encompasses a wide array of programs intended to prepare new teachers, including five-year university programs and graduate level university pre-service programs. It also includes a wide variety of non-university groups, such as Teach for America or Troops to Teachers. In some cases, school districts also develop programs to meet the high demand for qualified teachers in their schools.

The growth of alternative certification programs exploded in the 1980s in response to the growing concerns over teacher shortages. The idea for creating an alternative pathway to teaching was not a new one. As early as 1958, the Fund for the Advancement of Education of the Ford Foundation designed an alternative certification program that was implemented in the state of Arkansas (Lucas, 1996). It was designed in response to concerns about American education following the launching of Sputnik by the Soviet Union in October, 1957.

This early form of alternative certification did not spread nationally, however, and soon disappeared until others, like Teach for America, would take up the cause several decades later. The revival of alternative certification reform was more successful in the educational climate of the 1980s and 1990s where teacher shortages, concern over teacher quality, and even greater concern over failing urban schools were critical issues. Following the report of *A Nation at Risk* in 1983, the political and educational climate was right for reforms that attempted to provide additional teachers, especially to urban schools.

The number of states that permitted alternative certification grew rapidly during the late eighties and early nineties from eighteen in 1986 to forty in 1992 (Adelman, 1986; Feistritzer, 1985, 1990, 1993). New Jersey was the leader in proliferating alternative certification in the United States. In 1985, New Jersey developed the Provisional Teacher Certificate to address teacher shortages in the state (Grossman & Loeb, 2008).

New Jersey leads the United States with approximately 40 percent of the teachers in the state entering teaching through alternative certification routes (Feistritzer, 2008). Three states, New Jersey, California, and Texas, accounted for half of the teachers from alternative certification programs in the United States in 2005 (Feistritzer & Haar, 2008). Although it is far less common in most other states, it is a significant part of teacher preparation in the United States. There are an estimated 485 alternative certification programs in the United States (Feistritzer & Haar, 2008).

Although states vary drastically, the overall number of alternatively certified teachers in the United States has risen considerably in the past twenty years. In 1985, 275 teachers became certified in the United States through alternative certification (NCAC, 2008). In 1995, 6,932 teachers became certified through alternative certification. In 2005, 59,000 teachers became certified through alternative certification (NCAC, 2008).

Many colleges and universities in the United States have added to the alternative certification routes by creating graduate level pre-service teacher education programs. In 1999, approximately 30 percent of pre-service teachers already possessed a bachelor's degree and roughly two thirds of colleges and universities offered pre-service teacher education at the graduate level (Feistritzer, 1999). What began as a way of addressing the issue of teacher shortages soon became an established alternative to traditional four-year university pre-service teacher education in all fifty states.

Although there are many alternative certification programs, the most popular and most highly debated is Teach for America. Teach for America was created with the purpose of attracting talented college graduates into teaching and supplying much needed teachers to urban schools. Teach for America was founded in 1989 as an alternative certification process to the traditional university undergraduate pre-service teacher education program. Teach for America is the most visible and the most prolific alternative certification program in existence today.

Teach for America teachers receive training over a period of eight weeks during the summer prior to the school year they will begin teaching. The pre-service training includes a four-week national institute, a two-week local induction program, and observation and student teaching with experienced teachers during summer school (Kopp, 1994). The six weeks of classroom training offers various courses that are often taught by practicing teachers, some of whom began in the Teach for America program.

The training focuses heavily on the practical aspects of teaching such as classroom management and instructional strategies (Stoddart & Floden, 1989). Very little of the pre-service training is devoted to the theoretical foundations of learning, child development, or cultural issues of schooling in the United States (Stoddart & Floden, 1989). The new teachers receive continued professional development training and guidance from experienced teachers at several points during the school year.

As you might expect, Teach for America and other alternative certification programs have sparked much debate among educational professionals. Darling-Hammond, a professor of education at Stanford University wrote an article entitled *Who Will Speak for the Children? How 'Teach for America' Hurts Urban Schools and Students* that heavily criticizes the methods and results of the Teach for America program (Darling-Hammond, 1994b). Darling-Hammond emphatically questioned the approach and philosophy that college graduates, no matter how academically talented, can be prepared for the classroom in just eight weeks of summer training. She quoted the words of one Teach for America teacher to support this view.

I—perhaps like most TFAers—harbored dreams of liberating my students from public school mediocrity and offering them as good an education as I had received. But I was not ready. . . . As bad as it was for me, it was worse for the students. . . . Many of mine . . . took long steps on the path toward dropping out. . . . I was not a successful teacher and the loss to the students was real and large. (Darling-Hammond, 1994b, p. 21)

Darling-Hammond expressed great concern in her article that if Teach for America is doing a poor job of preparing teachers for the classroom, then it is doing a disservice to one of its primary objectives, to improve urban education (1994b).

Wendy Kopp, the founder of Teacher for America, replied to the charges made in the Darling-Hammond article that Teach for America is hurting students in urban schools (Kopp, 1994). In her response, Kopp pointed out that the quotation of the Teach for America teacher used in the article is only one opinion. The same opinions could be found in many beginning teachers coming from traditional university pre-service teacher education programs, especially those teaching at urban schools.

This view is supported by many educational professionals outside of Teach for America. One researcher stated, "In reality, neither traditionally nor alternatively certified teachers are prepared to meet the challenges of teaching in our most needy schools" (Zumwalt, 1996, p. 42). Obviously, the educational community has mixed feelings and opinions on the effectiveness of alternative certification programs, like Teach for America.

Without question, the most glaring fault of alternative certification is the shortened pre-service training period. Even though most teacher educators recognize that learning to teach is a life-long process that includes both pre-service and in-service teacher education, the limitations of preparing pre-service teachers in a shortened time period, such as the eight week training required by Teach for America, are undeniable. This one weakness may outweigh the multitude of strengths and positive contributions of alternative certification programs in the eyes of many teacher educators.

On the other hand, alternative certification programs such as Teach for America have many admirable qualities and strengths that are very noteworthy. One of the strengths of Teach for America is its success in attracting talented and diverse college graduates into teaching and into urban schools. Teach for America has traditionally recruited college graduates with excellent academic credentials. The grade point average (GPA) of Teach for America teachers averages 3.3 compared with emergency certified teachers, those given temporary certification due to a lack of certified teachers, whose average GPA is considerably lower at 2.41 (Dill, 1996).

A study by Humphrey and Wechsler of seven alternative certification programs found that alternative certification teachers were more likely to graduate from competitive colleges and universities than traditional teachers (2007). Teach for America achieves these results by recruiting at high level universities and through a selective application process where only 18 percent of applicants are accepted into the program (Kopp, 1994).

Furthermore, alternative certification programs have been successful at attracting individuals who might not otherwise enter the teaching profession. According to some researchers, Teach for America teachers are more likely to be older and come from a previous career than traditional university education majors (Dill, 1996). These second career teachers are especially common in science where it is estimated that 40 percent of the science teacher recruits were employed in a scientific job prior to entering Teach for America (Dill, 1996).

Feistritzer found this to be true for other alternative certification programs as well (2005). She found that 72 percent were thirty or older, 47 percent were forty or older, and 20 percent were fifty or older (Feistritzer, 2005). In the same study, Feistritzer found that 47 percent of people entering alternative certification programs had been working in a job outside of education the previous year and 40 percent were working in a professional occupation (2005).

Finally, the diversity of candidates entering the teaching profession through alternative certification programs is commendable. In their review of research on alternative certification, Wilson, Floden, and Ferrini-Mundy concluded that "alternative routes have successfully recruited a more diverse pool of teachers" (2002, p. 198). Although there were ethnic differences, Wilson, Floden, and Ferrini-Mundy found evidence that the socioeconomic status of teachers from alternative certification routes was very similar to traditional teachers (2002).

A more recent study by Feistritzer confirmed that alternative certification programs attracted more racially diverse teachers and found that 32 percent of early-entry alternative certification teachers were non-white (2005). Teach for America teachers include 40 percent people of color and 30 percent men as compared with the typical teacher workforce, which is 10 percent people of color and 20 percent men (Tatel, 1999).

As a reform, alternative certification programs such as Teach for America have raised important questions, addressed specific needs, and certainly altered the landscape of pre-service teacher education by offering an alternative to traditional university pre-service teacher education. The university-based system of pre-service teacher education had received plenty of criticism over its long history, but it had not been challenged by another route to teaching to this extent in the past fifty years.

The most common dissatisfaction with current university pre-service teacher education by teachers surveyed for this book was the lack of emphasis on practical issues of teaching and learning. Alternative certification routes, in general, are very practical. They rely upon practitioners and field experiences much more than traditional routes (Levine, 2006). So will teachers support alternative certification programs?

As a whole, the teachers surveyed were quite strongly opposed to alternative certification that placed teachers in classrooms with significantly less educational training. When asked if college graduates should be certified to teach in their field with no educational training, almost all teachers (97 percent) responded probably (23 percent) or definitely (74 percent) not. When asked if college graduates should be certified to teach with eight weeks of educational training, eight out of ten teachers (82 percent) responded probably (49 percent) or definitely (33 percent) not.

One middle school science teacher commented that the alternative certification training is "not fair to Ed [education] majors." Her feeling was that if the extended program of study and coursework was necessary for education majors in traditional programs, then it should be necessary for all. The converse may also be true. If it is not necessary for those in alternative programs, then perhaps it is not necessary for traditional programs either.

Because of how much each teacher preparation program varies, the research comparing alternative and traditional programs is mixed. The opinion of teachers, however, is not. Teachers in the field believe quite strongly that becoming a teacher takes an extended amount of preparation prior to one's first year of teaching.

On the other hand, the teachers surveyed were more accepting of nontraditional university-based programs that placed pre-service teacher education at the graduate level. Six out of ten teachers surveyed (56 percent) thought that pre-service teacher education should be offered at both the undergraduate and graduate level. The same middle school science teacher suggested graduate programs would help to attract more second career teachers. "We might be able to get teachers who have four year degrees that maybe didn't find their area rewarding enough and want to come into teaching," she said.

Although these teachers supported graduate level programs, they clearly did not want the graduate level programs to replace the traditional undergraduate programs. Just one in fifty teachers surveyed (2 percent) thought that pre-service teacher education should be offered at the graduate level only. There were some teachers (38 percent) that felt that pre-service teacher education should be offered only at the undergraduate level. Although this is a significant portion, the majority of teachers preferred that pre-service teacher education be offered at both the undergraduate and graduate level. The teachers' support for university-based alternative programs far exceeded the other more radical forms of alternative certification that exist outside of the university system.

Although teachers wanted a more practical pre-service teacher education experience, they were not ready to abandon the university programs that prepare teachers. Their opposition to alternative certification shows that the changes and reforms in teacher education should be more moderate and incremental. The emergence of alternative certification programs, and their fast-track approach to preparing teachers, may be an example of the pendulum swinging too far to correct for flaws, perceived or real, in traditional pre-service teacher education. Nonetheless, there may be important lessons to be learned from the alternative routes and their approaches to pre-service teacher education.

The answer as some see it is not to choose between traditional and alternative routes to teaching. "There may be value in ceasing to think of them as oppositional to one another. Perhaps the best course of action lies in blending these ideas, wherein the advantages of being close to practice are maintained, but so are the advantages of reflective and critical approaches to pedagogy" (Fenstermacher, 1990, p. 182). In other words, early-entry alternative certification programs may need to infuse more theoretical training into their practice-focused system of teacher preparation.

At the same time, traditional university pre-service teacher education programs must ensure that all aspects of their program, including university classroom courses, are closely connected to the practice of teaching and learning in today's school environments. The educational theory that is taught must inform and reflect upon the art and science of teaching that will be applied in the classroom by pre-service teachers.

According to Zeichner and Hutchinson, "Some advocates of traditional college and university preparation believe that 'reputable forms' of alternative certification may have a positive influence on traditional forms of teacher education by encouraging experimentation and innovation" (2008, p. 27). Zeichner and Hutchinson warned, "If we continue to seek evidence that any one model of teacher education is superior to others and to ignore the wide range of quality that exists within all models, we will continue to be disappointed in the results" (2008, p. 28). In this regard, research should search for lessons to be learned from all models of teacher education rather than act as a score keeper to the alternative certification debate.

Fenstermacher suggested that "being close to practice" is the lesson to be learned from alternative certification (1990, p. 182). If that is the case, then alternative certification reforms may have a tremendous effect on university pre-service teacher education. As it turns out, the teachers surveyed for this book agreed with this suggestion.

As you will read in the next chapter, the teachers surveyed supported several strategies to help teacher educators provide a more practical system for preparing new teachers. It may take a significant amount of time and effort on the part of university teacher educators and the willingness on the part of practicing teachers to get more involved, but it is a necessary step for creating the proper balance between theory and practice and improving the effectiveness and reputation of pre-service teacher education.

6

What Teachers Really Want
to Change about Teacher Education

One out of four teachers are mostly (22 percent) or very (3 percent) unsatisfied with the current state of pre-service teacher education. The most common reasons cited for this dissatisfaction were: a need for more practical preparation, bad experiences with student teachers, shortages or shortcomings of field experiences, poor preparation in classroom management, or the hoops required for certification. In addition, the teachers reported feeling unprepared for the following issues: classroom management, workload and paperwork, time management, parents, and administration and politics.

What should be changed to address these concerns? The feedback from teachers in the field provides a valuable starting point for an honest discussion about how to systemically and incrementally improve pre-service teacher education. What do teachers really want to change about teacher education? That is the question that will be addressed in this chapter.

The teachers surveyed were asked for their recommendations for pre-service teacher education. On this open-ended question, a total of 185 recommendations were provided by 103 different teachers. These comments were classified into eleven themes or categories, which are shown in figure 6.1 along with the number of comments for each theme. Throughout the survey, teachers were also asked several more specific questions about various changes or reforms to teacher education. These are the teachers' ideas for improving pre-service teacher education.

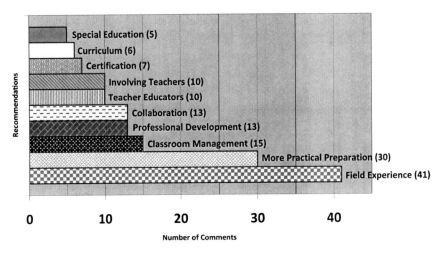

Figure 6.1.   Recommendations for Pre-Service Teacher Education

EXTENDED FIELD EXPERIENCES

The most common recommendation for improving pre-service teacher education given by elementary and secondary teachers was related to field experience. The survey and interview data both clearly indicated that teachers placed an enormous amount of value on what they learned from their field experiences. They clearly valued the field experience more than any of the university-based courses in pre-service teacher education. One middle school math teacher expressed this viewpoint:

> To be honest, I learned the most from being in the classrooms with other teachers, even if I was there just to observe. There is little in books that exceeds or even meets the value of actually having experiences with students and teacher in real classrooms. I took little away from my methods class, but gained *MUCH* more from other teachers and faculty.

A high school music teacher made a similar recommendation, and emphasized that the pedagogical knowledge could be taught in the context of a field experience.

> I can't emphasize enough the need for students to spend more time in actual K–12 classrooms working with teachers and students; as opposed to spending the time in a college classroom learning theory. . . . There is a specific

core of content and methods that must be conveyed prior to entering a classroom, but the majority of methodological and pedagogical content can be addressed in a more experientially based program while preservice teachers are in the classrooms.

Because of the value these teachers placed on their own field experience, their number one recommendation for pre-service teacher education was to increase the amount of field experience. One high school social studies teacher believed that more field experience would help future teachers to be better prepared. She said, "I have often commented that people leaving universities are not ready for the classroom (myself included!), but really had no answer for how to better prepare pre-service teachers. I think an answer could be, in general, more time in the classroom."

A high school math teacher added, "Even with the best classroom instruction, a teacher learns the most through interaction with a real live classroom. . . . The most emphasis in a preservice program should be in this area." One high school science teacher also recommended that field experiences "should start earlier in the program and be more integrated into courses."

A high school English teacher agreed that the field experiences could be better connected to the university coursework. She recommended that teacher educators should "integrate methods and management classes with student teaching experiences versus requiring all the classes before and only before student teaching."

Many of the issues for which teachers felt unprepared may arguably be issues that are best addressed in the context of meaningful field experiences. Where should pre-service teachers develop the knowledge and skills needed to manage their time, workload, paperwork, students, and classrooms? How will they learn to effectively communicate and collaborate with parents, administrators, or other teachers? While understanding human behavior and learning about theories of classroom management is something that can be taught at the university, it is the application of this knowledge that requires an authentic context. Not surprisingly then, one of the first things teachers would change about teacher education is the amount of field experience.

Some teachers recommended increasing the amount of field experience in pre-service teacher education. The vast majority of teachers in the survey (81 percent) had completed one semester of student teaching during their own pre-service teacher education. This is typical of most pre-service teacher education programs. While the teachers in the survey had completed 1.04 semesters of student teaching, on average, they recommended an average of 1.45 semesters of student teaching. Two out of five teachers (42 percent) suggested that student teachers should complete more than one semester of student teaching.

For one teacher that did not recommend increasing the amount of field experience, the reason was quite simple. "Education majors are already having such demands on getting them ready that very few are finishing in four years," explained a middle school science teacher. She believed that most university pre-service teacher education programs would not be able to remove a semester's worth of courses to keep the overall length of the program to less than four years.

As a result, adding field experience would likely add to the overall length of the program. She added, "I just don't think our profession is rewarding enough to require five years of education when their colleagues are going out getting a higher paying job." Her low estimation of the rewards of teaching was quite concerning, but she may have a point. Teaching is competing with other professions for the best candidates. In order to add rigor to teacher preparation, we may need to add more reward to the profession. She did note that she would be willing to add a semester of field experience, if the overall length of the program did not change.

The value that teachers place on field experience does not devalue the learning experiences that take place in the university classrooms. It only devalues those ideas that are taught in isolation of a meaningful context. If the knowledge and concepts learned at the university can be connected, developed, and applied in the field, then the pre-service teacher can find meaning in what they are learning at the university. If given multiple field placements throughout their preparation, then pre-service teachers are able to develop their knowledge and skills over time. This is important for any profession. In a profession where the first year professional is given the same responsibilities as a twenty year veteran, it is absolutely critical.

MORE PRACTICAL PREPARATION

The second most popular recommendation given by elementary and secondary teachers for improving pre-service teacher education was to provide more practical preparation. Recall, the number one dissatisfaction expressed by teachers was the need for more practical preparation. This common dissatisfaction was discussed in detail in the last chapter.

The desire for more field experience—which was the number one recommendation of teachers—may also relate to this perceived need for more practical preparation. One could argue that the most practical preparation occurs when knowledge and concepts are taught in the context of field experiences, where pre-service teachers are placed in K–12 classroom settings and given ample opportunity to understand and apply their understanding of the teaching and learning process.

In expressing their desire for more practical preparation, the teachers decried some of the elements of pre-service teacher education that seemed unrealistic or unauthentic. One middle and high school family and consumer science teacher suggested that pre-service teachers needed to be taught "realistic assessment and evaluation [techniques]—not just philosophical and ideal." The same teacher emphasized that pre-service teachers need "teaching strategies that work and that are realistic." She also explained that new teachers did not understand how to manage their time in the classroom, and that this skill need to be developed during pre-service teacher education, rather than during the first few years of teaching.

Some teachers expressed a concern that the most important responsibilities and strategies were given little attention in pre-service teacher education. One middle school teacher suggested that teacher educators are trying to cover too much. He recommended that teacher educators needed to "simplify" and "streamline" the curriculum in order to "focus on the meat and minimize [the] time spent on fluff." This would provide more time to address the truly important knowledge and skills that novice teachers need to be successful in the classroom.

A middle and high school French teacher echoed this concern, suggesting that pre-service teachers needed more time to master the basic responsibilities of a teacher. She explained, "When we get into the classroom, the things that were 'asides' in the ed program take up more time and attention than originally presented."

Truly, the pre-service teacher must develop the basic skills of planning, instructing, and assessing student learning just to survive their first year of teaching. Due to the limited time teachers are given to complete these tasks during a typical school day, the pre-service teachers must be very efficient at each of these tasks. The level of efficiency or mastery required of first year teachers is seldom practiced or realized during their pre-service preparation.

When it comes to planning lessons, several teachers thought the lesson plans created in pre-service teacher education were completely unrealistic. One high school Spanish teacher said, "I created many lesson plans throughout my career at the university, and to be honest I have not used one." She continued, "I wish we could have created unit plans that could have transferred over to my classroom."

One could argue that the role of pre-service teacher education is not to prepare lesson plans for future teaching. Nonetheless, teachers should know how to effectively plan lessons. If pre-service teachers are creating lessons that are unusable, will they be able to prepare effective lessons once they begin teaching? Pre-service teachers need to learn the thinking process that will allow them to plan effective lessons once they begin their teaching careers. Once again, given the limited time teachers are given to prepare lessons in a typical school day, this process must be thoroughly learned and rehearsed in pre-service teacher education so it can be accomplished with great efficiency in the field.

One middle school English teacher explained how the lengthy lesson plans required in some pre-service teacher education programs were exceedingly impractical. She recommended the following:

> Stop making students write fifty page lesson plans for everything they teach—or at least explain that this is not reality and they are just getting the "long way" to do it in college. No teacher in reality spends that much energy writing down everything they plan to say word for word. That's not real. Spend more time practicing with other classmates on how to teach, not what to teach.

Another teacher argued that having pre-service teachers complete these types of lengthy lessons plans led to problems for new teachers. According to this middle and high school French teacher, "This leads to either having to stay at school all night to create 'that fabulous lesson' that was the holy grail of the ed program or 'settling for less' and feeling ineffective." For these teachers, they encouraged teacher educators to help novice teachers develop a process for planning lessons that would be transferable to the real classroom, even if the lessons themselves were not.

To learn the roles and responsibilities of a teacher, a pre-service teacher must be asked to complete as many authentic tasks as possible during their pre-service preparation. One high school Spanish teacher complained, "I recall sitting through many lectures and not enough hands on [experiences]." Although the lectures may have been relevant, it could be that the pre-service teachers are unable to see the relevance until they are asked to apply it to an authentic task.

Pre-service teachers want to learn to do the types of things that teachers in the field are required to do. For that, a basic knowledge of theory and research is quite useful. Unfortunately, it only becomes practical when it can be applied under the same constraints that exist in a typical classroom.

Finally, several teachers also felt like their pre-service teacher education did not provide them with a true understanding of the teaching profession. One young high school social studies teacher suggested that teacher educators should "expose [the] rigors of [the] profession early." She admonished teacher educators to "quit pumpin' sunshine!" Perhaps, in her view, there were some issues—like paperwork, workload, or dealing with parents, administrators, or school politics—that were never identified or addressed in pre-service teacher education. These are the types of issues that a more practical pre-service preparation must address. Pre-service teachers need to be prepared for the rigors of the job or they will never enjoy its rewards.

MORE CLASSROOM MANAGEMENT, CONTENT, AND TEACHING METHODS

Although there are significant differences between pre-service teacher education programs, there are some common courses or topics that are generally addressed in almost all programs. While the names of the courses might be different, most pre-service teacher education programs include courses in the content or subject area being taught (e.g., art, math, science, etc.), the role of school in society (e.g., foundations of education), educational psychology, teaching methods, and classroom management, and others. In the survey, teachers were given these five course topics and asked if the amount of time devoted to each topic should be reduced, expanded, or stay the same.

These survey questions yielded a very interesting result. For all five topics, more teachers recommend that the amount of time devoted to each topic be expanded than reduced. This is similar to other public feedback and political pressure put on both K–12 schools and university schools of education. There is always more pressure to add new content and requirements for teachers and teacher education, without taking anything away.

As a result, elementary and secondary schools today offer a myriad of student services, including counselors, therapists, speech therapists, psychologists, translators, and others. While these all provide valuable services, most of the public is either unaware or unappreciative of these school related services. In higher education, this need to add or require more of teacher education has resulted in many undergraduate programs that require more than four years to complete and others that have moved pre-service teacher education to the graduate level.

Although the teachers recommended that more time and attention be given to all five topics, the amount of support for expanding each topic varied and provided an insight into teachers' views and priorities on these common components of pre-service teacher education. Based on these results, classroom management was the highest priority among teachers. Nine out of ten teachers (86 percent) recommended that the amount of time devoted to classroom management in pre-service teacher education be expanded.

This recommendation from teachers was consistently high regardless of age, gender, grade level taught, subject area taught, or graduate credits earned. This recommendation was also consistent with the teachers' responses to an earlier question, which asked teachers to identify what they were unprepared for as beginning teachers. The number one answer was classroom management.

One teacher said, "My program 'glossed over' classroom management." According to this middle school earth science teacher, "Without proper control teaching methods and lesson can become insignificant." As result, this teacher's recommendation for pre-service teacher education was to "hit on classroom management stronger." Another teacher, a high school English and social studies teacher, echoed this priority by recommending "as much exposure to classroom management as is possible."

A fifth grade teacher remarked, "Classroom management is huge." Sadly, this same teacher said, "I don't know that I ever heard anybody in college talk about that." Classroom management can entail many different issues, but is often equated with student behavior or discipline. One middle school teacher specifically cited student behavior as well as communication with parents, when she recommended that teacher education should "educate future teachers about how to deal with behavior issues and parental issues." Although student behavior is typically addressed in a classroom management course, communicating with parents may not be addressed at all in some pre-service programs.

In addition to managing student behavior, there are many other things that new teachers must learn to manage. These include: curriculum materials, paperwork, files, grading, facilities, technology, media, equipment, and supplies. These are often not addressed in a typical classroom management course.

This list is quite similar to the list of issues for which teachers reported feeling unprepared: classroom management, paperwork, workload, parents, organizing space, time management, administration, practical strategies, curriculum, grading, and lesson planning. Given the expressed need for more practical preparation, pre-service teacher education must prepare teachers for all of these management issues, whether through a classroom management course, another university course, or a field experience.

Obviously, classroom management was a major priority and concern for these veteran teachers. These teachers believed that pre-service teachers needed more time to learn and develop their knowledge and skills in this area, before beginning their first year of teaching. One young high school physical education teacher emphasized that new teachers "must be ready to take charge of a classroom."

In this respect, more time in the classroom with actual students during field experiences may also be helpful for developing the sort of assertiveness and professional disposition that is so vital in the classroom. An effective classroom presence cannot truly be developed in the university classroom. It can only be developed and practiced in the field, with the support and help of veteran teachers.

The next two largest priorities of teachers in pre-service teacher education were content area courses and teaching methods courses. Four out of ten teachers (42 percent) recommended that more time be spent on content or subject area courses (e.g., art, math, science, etc.). A high school technology education teacher suggested that pre-service teachers spend less time on education courses in order to "free up time to focus on content more." One high school social studies teacher recommended the opposite, more time in education courses and less time in content courses. She argued, "A good teacher can teach any subject." Her opinion, however, was in the minority,

Most teachers believed that there should be more time devoted to developing the content knowledge of pre-service teachers. The number of credits devoted to content courses and education courses will differ from one program to the next. Somehow, the right balance of content and education courses must be reached. According to teachers, most pre-service teacher education programs should focus more on developing content knowledge.

Interestingly, the research shows that the integration of content knowledge (knowing about the subject you teach) and pedagogical knowledge (knowing about the processes of teaching and learning) may be more important to overall teaching effectiveness. Shulman referred to this as pedagogical content knowledge (1986). In other words, teachers need to know how to design the curriculum and instruction in a specific subject area. In this way, the research may suggest that teachers need content courses that are better aligned to the content they will teach and education courses that are more specific to the subject they will teach.

Likewise, four out of ten teachers (40 percent) recommended that more time be spent on teaching methods. The recommendations for the amount of time devoted to methods courses in pre-service teacher education varied significantly by gender ($\chi^2(2, 189) = 10.80$, $p < .005$). Significantly more female teachers (49 percent) recommended expanding the amount of time devoted to methods courses than male teachers (27 percent).

The course topics that received the most recommendations for reducing the amount of time devoted were educational psychology and the role of school in society. Two out of ten teachers surveyed (18 percent) recommended that the amount of time devoted to educational psychology be reduced. Similarly, two out of ten teachers (17 percent) recommended that the amount of time devoted to the role of school in society be reduced. Based on the survey results, these courses are less valued by teachers than the courses on classroom management, content area, and teaching methods.

These results are consistent with teachers' dissatisfaction with pre-service teacher education programs that are too abstract or overly theoretical. In the course topics mentioned above, courses that focus on educational psychology and the role of school in society are typically more abstract and theoretical. It is in the role of school in society, or sometimes called foundations of education, that students study established philosophies of education that have influenced how our school system is designed and determines how a teacher approaches their role in schools. It is in educational psychology that pre-service teachers study the theories of learning, child development, and human behavior.

It is clear that these philosophies and theories of learning provide an underpinning to the roles and responsibilities of schools in society and school teachers in the classroom. These courses teach concepts that provide an important foundation for preparing teachers. In fact, the majority of teachers did not want to reduce the amount of time devoted to these topics. Instead, the majority of teachers surveyed recommended that the amount of time devoted to educational psychology (55 percent) and the role of school in society (53 percent) should stay the same.

On the other hand, it is clear that the teachers were more supportive of courses in classroom management, content, and teaching methods, and expanding the amount of time devoted to these areas. These are the courses that teachers would likely consider to be more practical. The content courses would be directly related to the topics the teachers would teach (e.g., art, math, science, etc.), especially for secondary school teachers. The classroom management and teaching methods courses would often include more of the practical tips and strategies that teachers may use on a daily basis in the classroom.

These recommendations from teachers may be more useful to teacher educators as a call to infuse a more practical and meaningful context into all teacher education courses, rather than a reflection of the value of each course. If the course is pragmatically taught with attention to the practical strategies that teachers can use to face the common challenges in learning and schooling, then teachers will find more value in it. Those courses that have historically been more successful at addressing the needs of practitioners should be expanded. Those courses that have been less attentive to the practical concerns of teachers should be revised to make the connections between theories and practice more evident to the novice teacher.

EXPERIENCE FOR TEACHER EDUCATORS

Another approach to addressing the need for more practical preparation can be found in the qualifications and experience of teacher educators. Today, many professors in university pre-service teacher education programs are also former teachers (Zeichner, 2003). A study by the National Center for Education Statistics found that 75 percent of university education faculty members have been employed outside of college or university positions, and 51 percent of those had their first non-university position in elementary or secondary schools (1999). Of course, not all teacher educators have experience in elementary or secondary schools. Should experience in K–12 schools be required for teacher educators?

The teachers surveyed were adamant that teacher educators should be required to have elementary or secondary teaching experience. In fact, twenty-four out of twenty-five teachers (96 percent) responded probably (29 percent) or definitely (67 percent) yes. When asked how many years should be required, the average number of years suggested was 5.45 years. The most common responses were five years, followed by three years, followed by ten years.

Interestingly, the older teachers recommended significantly less K–12 classroom experience than younger teachers ($F(3, 166) = 4.58$, $p < .005$). Teachers fifty years old and older recommended the fewest years of K–12 experience for teacher educators, an average of four years. By comparison, teachers between the ages of twenty-four and forty-nine recommended an average of six years of K–12 experience.

Perhaps, the older teachers better recognized the difficulties that a teacher with more experience may have in returning to graduate school to pursue a PhD, which is typically expected of a teacher educator or any university professor. At a certain point in life, becoming a graduate student with very modest income may not be financially feasible, especially for those supporting a family.

The results also showed a statistically significant difference based upon the number of graduate credits earned ($F(3, 152) = 3.54$, $p < .05$). The general trend showed that teachers with fewer graduate credits, particularly less than forty credits, suggested that teacher educators be required to have more years of K–12 teaching experience. Teachers with zero to thirty-nine graduate credits recommended six years of teaching experience. Teachers with forty or more graduate credits recommended five years of teaching experience. In light of this finding, it may be more important for teacher educators teaching pre-service or younger in-service teachers to have more K–12 classroom experience, at least from the perspective of the teachers themselves.

Clearly, the teachers surveyed felt that experience in elementary and secondary schools was essential for teacher educators. When asked for her recommendations for pre-service teacher education, one teacher encouraged university schools of education to "hire professors who have been in the classroom and have experience along with an open minded attitude to accept new ideas." This teacher, and many others, believed that it was essential for someone to have experience in K–12 schools in order to be qualified to teach K–12 teachers, pre-service or in-service.

An elementary teacher said, "If a teacher is going to teach me how to teach kids, they have to have done it." A high school technology education teacher stated that "university faculty needs to see the real world that they are sending teachers into." For this teacher, the need for K–12 school experience was directly tied to the recommendation that pre-service teacher education needed to be more practical. He continued, "University faculty many times take an idealistic approach to the classroom and not a practical approach."

One high school foreign language teacher frankly stated, "I would respect someone much more if he teaches education classes and I know this person has taught for many years." By contrast, if the person did not have experience at the K–12 level, she said she would ask, "Well, how do you know that?" For this teacher, it was an issue of credibility. The same teacher suggested that teacher educators should be able to "talk to students [pre-service teachers] about your experiences [in elementary or secondary school classrooms]." She believed that sharing personal stories, experiences, and strategies from the teacher educators' own experience would benefit pre-service teachers.

Another teacher explained her support by saying, "I am thinking that you will be a better professor if you have a feeling for what an elementary classroom is like versus a high school classroom and the teaching that is done." She believed that experience at the elementary and secondary level would be a "reality check" for teacher educators, which may help prepare more relevant and practical experiences for pre-service teachers.

For this middle school science teacher, it was also important that the teacher educators have experience at the grade span for which their students (pre-service teachers) are being prepared. She commented, "I do have some high school teacher friends and I have taught in the elementary, and they are two entirely different balls [games]."

These teachers recognized that the instructors in pre-service teacher education programs were vitally important and critical factors in the success or failure of pre-service teacher education. Another middle and high school technology education teacher said, "Great instructors model what good teachers do. The curriculum is not taught, but lived out." From this perspective, if pre-service teachers are to be prepared effectively, they must be taught by teacher educators who can model the best practices seen in elementary and secondary classrooms.

The idea that teachers want teacher educators to have K–12 classroom experience may not be surprising. What is surprising is that teachers overwhelming believed it should be required. What is even more surprising is that teachers also overwhelmingly believed that it was important for teacher educators to return to the K–12 classroom periodically during their career as teacher educators.

Nine out of ten teachers thought that teacher educators should probably (43 percent) or definitely (43 percent) return to the K–12 classroom periodically during their tenure as education professors. When asked how often teacher educators should return to the classroom, the average number recommended was every 4.97 years. The most common response was every five years, followed by every three years, followed by every ten years.

Teacher educators do frequently spend time in K–12 classrooms on a variety of collaborative projects, including research and professional development projects. These experiences and partnerships with teachers can help teacher educators better understand the practical issues that teachers face every day. However, these experiences don't typically involve teaching a full day in a K–12 classroom. They certainly don't involve teaching at the K–12 school for a full semester or year.

Such an arrangement could have many benefits to teacher educators and teacher education, but it also has numerous obstacles. Based on their level of education, a school would likely need to pay significantly more to hire a PhD to a K–12 teaching position. Given the limitations of the current K–12 budgets, not many schools would elect to pay more. In addition, a university faculty member might have to leave their position at the university, without a guarantee of being hired back later. If they were hired back later, the time away from the university may make promotion and tenure at the university more difficult. The logistics and job uncertainty may make these periodic job changes very difficult.

Although there are many obstacles, there are some opportunities for teacher educators to return to K–12 practice, while keeping their position at the university. Jill Fox, a professor of early childhood education at the University of Texas at Arlington, arranged and participated in a job-sharing experience with a kindergarten teacher at a nearby professional development school (2006). Both she and the teacher retained their positions, salary, and benefits at their respective schools.

In the arrangement, Fox taught kindergarten on Mondays, Tuesdays, and Wednesdays and worked at the university on Thursdays and Fridays. The kindergarten teacher taught a university course and supervised student teachers on Mondays and Tuesdays and taught kindergarten on Wednesdays, Thursdays, and Fridays. They shared the kindergarten teaching responsibilities on Wednesday so that they could communicate and transition between the two jobs.

Fox had taught kindergarten in public schools for eight years before pursuing her PhD degree and beginning a career in teacher education. Fox noted several surprises upon returning to the elementary school classroom as a kindergarten teacher (2006). First, she stated, "I realized changes in my own perspectives after years in higher education" (Fox, 2006, p. 243). She had forgotten about "potty problems, playground injuries, nosebleeds, lost teeth, [and] runny noses" (Fox, 2006, p. 244). Fox also noted that several things had changed since she had taught kindergarten, including the use of latex gloves, students' lack of familiarity with units of money and coins in particular, and classroom technology (Fox, 2006).

Although Fox had a positive and valuable learning experience in the kindergarten classroom, she reported that the job-share experience had a negative effect on her post-tenure review. Although she considered the experience to be a scholarly activity, it was determined that she had done no scholarly activity during that year because she had not published during the year (Fox, 2006). Unfortunately, the obstacles to this type of arrangement are real.

In order for teacher-teacher educator partnerships to be effective, peers and administrators at the school and university must value the important benefits of these types of collaborations. While sabbaticals are typically granted to pursue research or other scholarly activities, they could also be used for teacher educators to return to the K–12 classroom. This would provide a great value for teacher educators and teacher education.

At the same time, the job share described above provided an opportunity for a teacher to work temporarily at the university as a teacher educator. In fact, this is another approach to addressing the need for more practical preparation in pre-service teacher education. This brings us to the next recommendation from teachers, that teachers be more involved in pre-service teacher education.

INCREASED TEACHER INVOLVEMENT

The teachers surveyed also advocated for the increased involvement of elementary and secondary teachers in pre-service teacher education. One middle school music teacher remarked, "I like the concept of teachers or 'master' teachers being used in the undergraduate classroom to give views and knowledge to preservice teachers." Instead of bringing teacher educators back to K–12 schools, this approach brings K–12 teachers to the university.

An elementary teacher suggested that "incorporating more regular education teachers in preservice teacher education programs would benefit all participants." This implies the belief that pre-service teachers, in-service teachers, and teacher educators might all benefit from the increased collaboration and involvement of elementary and secondary teachers in pre-service teacher education.

Once again, the support of this strategy is grounded in the teachers' beliefs that pre-service teacher education should be more relevant and practical. One middle school English and social studies teacher explained that pre-service teacher education would benefit from "more communication between university staff and teachers regarding what's relevant and important for teaching." The determination of what is relevant and important for pre-service teachers to know and experience is best done in collaboration, not isolation of one another.

Veteran teachers could utilize their classroom experience to help pre-service teachers make the important connections between theory and practice. Practicing teachers may be more attentive to the practical tips and strategies that pre-service teachers would find helpful. The veteran teachers may also help the pre-service teachers make valuable connections between what they learn in the university classroom and what they experience in the field. A high school mathematics teacher, suggested that veteran teachers "should be used as supervisors by the university [during field experiences]."

The traditional approach to involving practicing teachers in pre-service teacher education is during field experiences in the role of a cooperating teacher. According to research, cooperating teachers have an enormous amount of influence on the development of pre-service teachers in this role (Glickman & Bey, 1990; Calderhead & Shorrock, 1997; Toll, Nierstheimer, Lenski, & Kolloff, 2004). Some researchers have even concluded that cooperating teachers are the most influential figure in the preparation of pre-service teachers because of their close relationship with the student teacher (Richardson-Koehler, 1988; American Association, 1991).

Yet, the involvement of cooperating teachers is generally limited to the field experience component of pre-service teacher education. Although this is a very influential component of pre-service teacher education, it leaves a large portion of pre-service teacher education relatively unaffected by the involvement of practicing teachers. Teachers could contribute to teacher preparation in many other ways, beyond the traditional role of the cooperating teacher.

In general, teachers strongly supported more teacher involvement in pre-service teacher education. When asked if they thought practicing teachers and their ideas should be more involved and influential in pre-service teacher education, nine out of ten teachers surveyed (85 percent) responded probably (55 percent) or definitely yes (30 percent). By comparison, just one in thirty teachers (3 percent) responded probably not (3 percent) or definitely not (0 percent).

Once again, the results varied significantly based upon the number of graduate credits earned, $F(3, 167) = 5.44$, $p < .001$. Those teachers who had completed the fewest number of graduate credits, less than thirty, expressed the least support for more teacher involvement ($M = 3.79$, $SD = 0.83$).

Teachers with thirty to thirty-nine graduate credits (M = 4.15, SD = 0.63), forty to fifty-nine graduate credits (M = 4.34, SD = 0.57), and sixty or more graduate credits (M = 4.27, SD = 0.69) were significantly more supportive of increasing teacher involvement in pre-service teacher education.

One possible explanation for this may be that teachers with fewer graduate credits feel less qualified or less interested in participating in pre-service teacher education. As teachers gain more experience, they may feel more compelled and more qualified to become involved in preparing new teachers. In reality, it is the teachers with more experience that would be recruited to become more involved in teacher preparation anyway.

Clearly, teachers would like to see elementary and secondary teachers more involved in pre-service teacher education. This begs the question: In what ways can teachers become more involved? One of the most obvious approaches to teacher involvement is through regular meetings with university teacher educators.

In order to determine how often teachers are involved in pre-service teacher education (beyond the traditional role of the cooperating teacher), the survey asked teachers if they had ever meet with teacher educators regarding pre-service teacher education. Approximately one-third of teachers surveyed (32 percent) had met with university faculty members to discuss the teacher education program.

When you consider the logistical, geographical, and time constraints that could make the arrangement of these meetings difficult, the number of teachers who had met with university faculty members was quite remarkable. Moreover, it would not be necessary for teacher educators to meet with every teacher in their area to gain their perspective and feedback on the practices and issues of the program.

When teachers were asked if they would be willing to meet with university faculty to discuss the teacher education program, nine out of ten teachers (95 percent) indicated that they would maybe (23 percent), probably (42 percent), or definitely (30 percent) be willing to meet. In fact, some teachers described these types of meetings as a necessity for teachers and teacher educators. One high school mathematics teacher stated, "Universities and local schools need to have a strong relationship for the sharing of ideas."

A high school French and English as a second language (ESL) teacher expressed her support by saying, "I believe dialogue between cooperating teachers, university school of ed faculty, and arts and sciences faculty would be best." While these types of collaborations and partnerships are valued by both teachers and teacher educators, they are more difficult to arrange and maintain due to the time constraints and logistics involved for both parties. As a result, the belief in partnerships is often more pervasive than the partnerships themselves.

As a whole, teachers are very willing to support their local pre-service teacher education programs through the sharing of ideas at regular meetings. By gender, female teachers were significantly more willing to meet with university faculty than male teachers (t(137) = –2.08, p < .05). This is consistent with earlier findings that showed that female teachers rated their pre-service teacher education experience more highly, reported using more methods from the university methods course, and showed greater support for professional development schools and standards-based reform.

Finally, when asked if regular meetings between practicing teachers and university faculty members would benefit or improve pre-service teacher education, nine out of ten teachers (90 percent) said that regular meetings would be somewhat (27 percent), quite (47 percent), or very (16 percent) beneficial to pre-service teacher education. Together, the results of this survey indicate a strong willingness and support among teachers for regular meetings between teachers and teacher educators to discuss the teacher education program.

In addition to regular meetings, how else could teachers become more involved in pre-service teacher education? One strategy would be to involve teachers in teaching or co-teaching university education courses. One high school foreign language teacher thought "the students [pre-service teachers] would benefit from that a lot." She explained, "Our teachers have so much experience . . . I have a plethora of information and my colleagues too, and resources, that students would really enjoy."

Although this practice is not widespread in university schools of education, it has become slightly more popular with the emergence of professional development schools in the 1990s. When Lee Teitel of the University of Massachusetts at Boston conducted studies on professional development schools in 1990, and again in 1995, he found several examples where universities used teachers from professional development schools to co-teach university education courses (Teitel, 1997).

In 1998, Rowan University in Glassboro, New Jersey, permanently moved two required undergraduate education courses to a professional development school site (McBee & Moss, 2002). Placing university education courses at the school site allows teachers to be more easily involved as a co-teacher or guest speaker and, at the same time, allows teacher educators to have a greater presence in the K–12 schools (McBee & Moss, 2002). As a result, even teachers who do not co-teach the university education courses might still have a better awareness and larger role in pre-service education courses.

At the University of Colorado at Denver, selected teachers have been given university positions as "Teachers in Residence" to co-teach courses in education on campus and supervise student teachers as university supervisors (Levine, 2002, p. 67). Although many teacher educators have invited teachers to participate in education courses as guest speakers, the creation of positions for teachers in teacher preparation gives teachers a more permanent position on campus. These positions also provide formal systems on campus for dealing with the logistics of time commitments and compensation.

Another university even created a "teacher exchange" program between the university and a professional development school where practicing teachers taught in university undergraduate education courses while university faculty members and graduate students worked and taught in their K–12 classrooms (Sharpe, 1992; Sharpe et al., 1994; Sharpe et al., 1995). This program allowed teachers to become more involved in the instruction of university education courses and created an opportunity for teacher educators to gain additional knowledge and experience about classroom conditions and issues in teaching and learning.

Another extraordinary example is the "Visiting Teaching Lecturer" program at the University of Western Sydney-Macarthur in Australia (Perry, Dockett, Kember, & Kuscher, 1999). This program began in 1992 and invites practicing teachers with at least four years of teaching experience and reputations for exemplary teaching to work in the university pre-service teacher education program for one year. The teachers remain under contract with the school district and are paid the salary they would have received in their normal teaching assignment for that year (Perry, Dockett, Kember, & Kuscher, 1999). The university then reimburses the school district for the salary of the teacher (Perry, Dockett, Kember, & Kuscher, 1999).

The founders of the program cited the importance of connecting theory and practice as one reason for beginning the program. They stated that the "place of the practicum [student-teaching] in teacher education is well accepted . . . , but it is no longer considered to be sufficient to enable the links between theory and practice to be made adequately" (Perry, Dockett, Kember, & Kuscher, 1999, p. 384).

They went on to say that "differences in the nature of knowledge about teaching held by classroom teachers and academics were expected, but regarded as differences rather than deficiencies" and that "the opportunity to combine the varying strengths of procedural knowledge of classroom teachers with the more declarative knowledge of university lecturers was regarded as one of the strengths of the programme" (Perry, Dockett, Kember, & Kuscher, 1999, p. 383). Clearly, the teacher educators in this example considered the practical knowledge of classroom practitioners as complementary to the more theoretical and evidence-based knowledge of the university faculty, rather than oppositional to it.

According to the researchers, the inclusion of teachers as visiting faculty was also reported to "add credibility" to the pre-service teacher education program in the eyes of its students (Perry, Dockett, Kember, & Kuscher, 1999, p. 388). Overall, the visiting teaching lecturer program received positive reviews from students, faculty, and teachers. The researchers concluded that the program had been "beneficial for all involved" (Perry, Dockett, Kember, & Kuscher, 1999, p. 391).

Unfortunately, the program was cancelled in 1996 for logistical reasons when the Department of School Education reorganized from regional offices to smaller district offices (Perry, Dockett, Kember, & Kuscher, 1999). The University of Western Sydney–Macarthur also expressed financial hardships on the part of the university as another reason for not continuing the program. A similar program was later reinstituted with one semester visiting faculty positions rather than full year positions.

In the spring of 2000, the University of Wisconsin-Milwaukee developed and implemented a similar program, called the "Teacher-in-Residence (TIR)" program, to involve teachers from urban schools in pre-service teacher education (Post, Pugach, Harris, & Hedges, 2006, p. 211). The initial program was funded by a Title II: Teacher Quality Enhancement Grant from the U.S. Department of Education and involved nineteen veteran teachers from the Milwaukee Public Schools (Post et al., 2006). Unfortunately, funding is often one of the obstacles to these types of partnerships.

The teachers-in-residence were given the charge of establishing better connections between the curriculum and instruction of the pre-service teacher education program and "urban classroom practice" (Post et al., 2006, p. 212). Teachers-in-residence were assigned a variety of different roles and responsibilities in the pre-service teacher education program.

Some teachers-in-residence served as "full members of an instructional team" in the school of education which included "co-teaching preservice courses with UWM faculty" (Post et al., 2006, p. 219). Others were involved in placing students in appropriate field placements, supervising students in these placements, co-teaching courses with content faculty, revising general education courses, recruiting students of color, or other various assignments (Post et al., 2006).

The teacher-in-residence program experienced many challenges as well as successes. The first challenge was the culture shift required for teachers-in residence to move from the K–12 environment to the university setting (Post et al., 2006). The teachers-in-residence had to adjust to the schedule of the university and the lack of clearly defined tasks or periods by managing their own time and setting their own priorities. The lack of structure initially frustrated some of the teachers-in-residence. The university faculty responded to this concern by giving the teachers-in-residence more clearly defined tasks and objectives.

The teacher-in-residence program appears to have affected both the university and the teachers who participated in significant ways. There were many changes to the curriculum and instruction of general education courses, content courses, professional education courses, and many other facets of the pre-service teacher education program, as discussed above. According to Post, Pugach, Harris, and Hedges, the teachers-in-residence were also able to "bring expertise and experience in urban schools as well as gain a much more informed understanding of teacher preparation" (2006, p. 217).

The program also affected the teachers significantly. One teacher-in-residence remarked, "It really pushed us to explore the broader context and reflect on ourselves as professional educators" (Post et al., 2006, p. 227). Post, Pugach, Harris, and Hedges, also identified the teacher leadership institute as one of the strengths of the program (2006). They believed that developing teacher leaders in the schools was a very worthwhile and productive approach to urban school reforms (Post et al., 2006).

Many other universities are successfully involving teachers from professional development schools and cooperating schools by teaching and co-teaching university education courses. These universities have set an important precedent for the involvement of teachers in the university-based component of pre-service teacher education. Although the involvement of teachers in teaching and co-teaching university education courses offers promising benefits, the practice has not yet entered the mainstream of pre-service teacher education.

There are many challenges to this level of teacher involvement, including philosophical, economical, and logistical hurdles. The few exemplary examples discussed above have shown enormous benefits and promise. Are teachers willing to become involved in teacher preparation in these ways?

In the survey, teachers were asked about teaching or co-teaching university education courses as guest instructors, part-time instructors, and full-time instructors and if they thought such practices would be beneficial. When asked if they had ever taught a university education course, one in ten teachers (9 percent) had taught or co-taught a university education course. Once again, when you consider the logistical, geographical, and time constraints that could make the arrangement of these teaching assignments difficult, this is a remarkable number and a positive sign that teacher involvement in pre-service teacher education is already taking place.

While one in ten teachers surveyed had taught or co-taught a university education course, there were many more teachers who would be willing to do so. In fact, eight out of ten teachers surveyed (80 percent) indicated they would maybe (22 percent), probably (29 percent), or definitely (29 percent) be willing to occasionally guest teach a university education course. This shows a surprising willingness on the part of teachers to become more involved in teacher preparation.

The willingness of teachers to guest teach varied significantly based on gender ($t(143) = -3.48$, $p < .001$) and subject area ($F(8, 180) = 2.05$, $p < .05$). By gender, female teachers were significantly more willing to guest teach university education courses than male teachers. By subject area, teachers in music, foreign language, English as a second language (ESL), and English were significantly more willing to guest teach than teachers in social studies, science, and math.

Would the same teachers be willing to teach regularly as a part-time instructor? Overwhelmingly, the answer is yes. Seven out of ten teachers (73 percent) indicated they would maybe (27 percent), probably (25 percent), or definitely (21 percent) be willing to teach university education courses part-time. Once again, female teachers were significantly more willing to teach or co-teach university education courses part-time on a regular basis than male teachers (t(186) = −3.08, p < .005).

As a follow-up question, the teachers who had responded maybe, probably, or definitely yes were asked about the types of compensation they would accept for teaching university education courses as a part-time instructor. Nine out of ten teachers (90 percent) would accept a part-time instructor's salary, five out of ten teachers (51 percent) would accept graduate credit, and four out of ten (43 percent) would accept a reduction in K–12 teaching duties as compensation.

Teachers fifty years of age and older (33 percent) were significantly less willing to accept graduate credits as compensation than teachers between the ages of 24 and 29 (65 percent), 30 and 39 (59 percent), or 40 and 49 (59 percent), $\chi^2(3, 140) = 8.74$, p < .05. This is likely due to the financial structure of teacher salaries where younger teachers would benefit more from an increase in graduate credits on the pay scale.

The percentage of teachers who would accept a reduction in K–12 teaching duties as compensation also varied significantly by age ($\chi^2(3, 140) = 12.09$, p < .01). Teachers between the ages of 30 and 39 (59 percent) and 40 and 49 (54 percent) were significantly more likely to accept a reduction in K–12 teaching as compensation. On the other hand, teachers between the ages of 24 and 29 (25 percent) and 50 and over (29 percent) were less likely to accept a reduction of K–12 teaching as compensation. The youngest and oldest teachers were much more interested in salary than a reduction in teaching load. It's likely the youngest teachers are trying to pay off student loans, while the oldest teachers may be trying to boost the formula used to calculate retirement benefits.

Are teachers also interested in teaching or co-teaching full-time for one year? Again, the answer is overwhelmingly yes. The results showed that seven out of ten teachers (72 percent) would maybe (27 percent), probably (19 percent), or definitely (26 percent) be willing to teach university education courses for one year for their current salary and benefits if they were guaranteed to be able to return to their K–12 teaching position the following year.

The responses varied significantly by age ($F(3, 181) = 4.79$, $p < .005$) and subject area ($F(8, 178) = 2.00$, $p < .05$). Teachers under forty years of age were significantly more likely to be willing to teach full-time at the university than teachers over forty. By subject area, teachers in foreign language, English as a second language, multiple subjects, and English were significantly more willing to teach full-time for one year than teachers in technology education, science, and math. Further research is needed to explain why these differences exist.

Finally, teachers were asked about a teacher-faculty exchange program where teachers teach university education courses full-time and teacher educators teach in the K–12 classroom full-time for one year. Seven out of ten teachers surveyed (73 percent) would probably (51 percent) or definitely (22 percent) support a teacher-faculty exchange program. Interestingly, this question did not produce any significant differences based on gender or subject area, as the previous questions had yielded.

Overall, the results of the survey indicated a strong willingness and support among teachers for teacher involvement in pre-service teacher education in a variety of different roles. Teachers are willing to meet with university teacher educators, guest teach, teach part-time, teach full-time, and participate in faculty-teacher exchanges. These results are very encouraging for teacher educators who may be seeking ways to involve teachers.

Teachers supported these types of strategies and believed they would benefit pre-service teacher education immensely. Nine out of ten teachers (92 percent) thought it would be somewhat (24 percent), quite (46 percent), or very (22 percent) beneficial to pre-service teacher education. Of course, the perceived benefit also varied by subject area ($F(8, 176) = 2.35$, $p < .05$). Those teachers in music, multiple subjects, and English were more likely to think that teacher involvement would be beneficial than those in social studies, math, and technology education.

7

Meet the Teachers Satisfied with Their Teacher Education Experience

In order to better understand what teachers really think about teacher education, some of the elementary and secondary teachers who participated in the survey were also selected to be interviewed. This allowed for a more personal and in-depth conversation on pre-service teacher education. These conversations allowed the teachers to not only share their views on pre-service teacher education, but also to share the reasoning behind their views.

The interview included a list of twenty-seven prepared questions (appendix B), which explored similar topics to the survey and allowed a more open-ended response. More importantly, it allowed the teachers to share their thoughts and beliefs about pre-service teacher education in general. In many cases, the teachers shared their insights and recommendations much more openly in the interview. These conversations were a valuable opportunity for teachers to share their ideas with one teacher educator, and a valuable opportunity for one teacher educator to share their thoughts with you.

Based on a factor analysis of the survey results, there were found to be four different types of teachers in the survey sample. The teachers were purposively selected from the survey sample to represent these four different groups of teachers. The four groups were teachers who were:

1. Satisfied with their own pre-service teacher education, and willing to be involved.

2. Satisfied with their own pre-service teacher education, but unwilling to be involved.
3. Dissatisfied with their own pre-service teacher education, but willing to be involved.
4. Dissatisfied with their own pre-service teacher education and unwilling to be involved.

The individual teachers in these four groups tended to respond to many different questions in very similar ways. Interviewing just a couple of teachers from a particular group provided insights into the perspective of that group of survey respondents. Therefore, two teachers from each group were selected to be interviewed. The four groups of teachers and pseudonyms for the teachers are listed below in table 7.1.

In this chapter, you will meet four teachers who were all satisfied with their pre-service teacher education experience. Two were willing to become more involved in pre-service teacher education and two were not. Ms. Foster and Ms. Wallace were satisfied with their pre-service teacher education experience and expressed a willingness to become involved. While Mr. Clark and Mr. Cook were both satisfied with their pre-service teacher education experience, they were unwilling to become involved themselves. This chapter will share their stories, ideas, and beliefs.

MEET MS. FOSTER: A SIXTH GRADE TEACHER

Ms. Foster teaches science and reading to sixth grade students at a fairly large middle school in Wisconsin. Interestingly, she teaches in the same district as Ms. Nelson. Ms. Foster is a forty-seven-year-old Caucasian female with twenty-one years of teaching experience and fifty graduate

Table 7.1.   Four Groups of Teachers

	Satisfied with Their Teacher Education Experience	*Dissatisfied with Their Teacher Education Experience*
Willing to be Involved	Ms. Foster	Mr. Gray
	Ms. Wallace	Ms. Kraft
Unwilling to be Involved	Mr. Clark	Mr. Ford
	Mr. Cook	Ms. Nelson

credits. The interview with Ms. Foster took place sitting at a small table in her classroom.

Ms. Foster was generally satisfied with her own pre-service teacher education experience. In the survey, Ms. Foster rated her own pre-service teacher education experience as very good (a four on a five point scale). She attended a traditional undergraduate pre-service teacher education program at a public Midwestern university, and later completed her master's degree in education. She reported that her pre-service teacher education experience was mostly relevant (a four on a five point scale) and that she felt mostly prepared (a four on a five point scale). The only thing she reported feeling unprepared for was "classroom management."

In the interview, Ms. Foster explained that her pre-service teacher education program "did a real nice job of getting me ready for my teaching experience." She felt that learning to design daily and unit lesson plans that were "teachable" was the most valuable part of her pre-service experience. During the interview, she also described the weakness of her preparation. "I do not feel I was ready for the behavioral concerns," she said. She also explained that she was not ready for some of the "cultural differences" that existed at the school, where she began her teaching career.

Although she was satisfied with her own pre-service preparation, Ms. Foster did not feel the same way about current pre-service teacher education programs. In the survey, she reported that she was mostly unsatisfied (a two on a five point scale) with current pre-service teacher education programs. She believed there was a significant gap (a four on a five point scale) between the theories taught in these programs and the practices of teachers in the field. She based her opinion, in part, on her experiences working as a cooperating teacher with five student teachers.

In the interview, she explained why she was unhappy with the student teachers, and by extension dissatisfied with the quality of the pre-service teacher education program. She explained, "I felt they were not prepared to create their own lessons and put their personality into it." This was something that she had learned to do in her own pre-service preparation, but was lacking with the student teachers with whom she had worked. She complained that the student teachers "didn't have enough experience putting together a lesson that wasn't outside the teacher manual."

Ms. Foster said, "They [the student teachers] were more interested in a textbook approach to teaching it, and I hadn't been doing that." Later in the interview, she remarked that the student teachers would "open up the book, teach the lesson, close it up, and be done." According to Ms. Foster, this is not acceptable in her current practice. She explained, "We're being asked now in the current classrooms to give them a tie to their real life or to some sort of outside program and our textbooks aren't doing that." According to Ms. Foster, this was the reason that she had reported a significant gap between what is taught in pre-service programs and what is practiced in schools.

While criticizing their ability to effectively plan lessons, she complimented the content knowledge of the student teachers. "They knew the subject matter really well, but they weren't able to make it age appropriate and interesting," she said. In addition, she also felt the student teachers did "not have very good time management skills," a quality that she felt was important to their success during student teaching.

Although she was mostly unsatisfied with her local pre-service teacher education program, and the quality of its student teachers, Ms. Foster was willing to be involved. When asked in the survey if teachers and their ideas should be more involved in pre-service teacher education, she responded definitely yes (a five on a five point scale), and that she was definitely willing (a five on a five point scale) to meet with university faculty members. In fact, she had done so before. She believed such meetings would be very beneficial (a five on a five point scale).

In the interview she reported that she had met with university faculty members before and felt it had been helpful. She explained that there needed to be a "good exchange or camaraderie" between teachers and teacher educators. She felt that teacher educators could find successful teachers to help inform how pre-service teachers are taught to teach in university programs.

She also felt that teachers in the field could bring issues or challenges to university faculty members to seek their counsel and expertise. In her view, a closer relationship between teachers and teacher educators could help student teachers be better prepared for the classroom and possibly reduce the number of new teachers that leave the profession in the first few years of teaching.

In addition to supporting regular meetings, Ms. Foster also believed that teachers could be involved in teaching education courses in pre-service teacher education. When asked if she would be willing to guest teach for a day, teach on a regular part-time basis at the university, or even teach full-time for one year at the university, Ms. Foster replied definitely yes (a five on a five point scale) to all three questions. She believed that involving elementary and secondary teachers in this way would be very beneficial (a five on a five point scale) to pre-service teacher education.

Ms. Foster had recently taught summer courses for in-service teachers before and believed that she benefited greatly from the experience. During the interview, Ms. Foster shared that she was "not at all interested in going [into] the administrative area" because she loves teaching too much. She viewed becoming involved in pre-service or in-service teacher education as a more desirable professional advancement opportunity. She stated, "If I knew I could take a year or two off and come back, I probably would go teach at a college."

During the interview, Ms. Foster made several recommendations for pre-service teacher education. First, she believed that pre-service teachers needed more preparation for working with students with special needs. According to Ms. Foster, new teachers must be capable of "challenging the exceptional students and challenging the lower ability students." Second, Ms. Foster recommended that pre-service teachers must develop better "time management" skills. Third, she felt that pre-service teachers needed better "classroom management" skills. In regards to developing time management and classroom management skills, she added, "It has to be in the field."

After coding the interviews, certain themes emerged from each interview. During this chapter and the next, a theme will be identified for each interview. This is helpful to understand the basis for the views and beliefs expressed by each individual teacher. When the views and beliefs are compared across all eight interviews, it helps to provide a theoretical framework to better understand what teachers truly value in pre-service teacher education.

The interview with Ms. Foster revolved around one major theme, her experience with student teachers and her concerns about their preparation. She used her experience in working with five student teachers to support many of the views and suggestions she expressed in the interview. In many ways, she felt that her student teachers were unprepared to teach effectively.

First, she observed that many of her student teachers were "more interested in a textbook approach to teaching." According to Foster, the student teachers also had a difficult time providing students with a "tie to their real life." To address these types of issues, Ms. Foster believed that cooperating teachers needed to know what has or has not been taught in the pre-service teacher education program "because then I know when I get the student teacher, she really has not had much on building a theme, applying current learning to current curriculum, and so I know that's what I need to do."

Second, Foster observed that most student teachers "did not have very good time management skills." They were unable to effectively manage the class's time or their own. She also observed student teachers struggle with classroom management issues. As a new teacher, Ms. Foster also remembered feeling unprepared for "behavioral issues."

However, she believed classroom management could be learned during field experiences. She stated, "I think you can have classroom management, pick that up as you go, as long as your time management works." Although she thought much could be learned in the field, she favored just one semester of student teaching. She stated, "I just don't think our profession is rewarding enough to require five years of education when their colleagues are going out getting a higher paying job."

MEET MS. WALLACE: A GERMAN TEACHER

Ms. Wallace teaches German and English to ninth through twelfth grade students at a large high school in Wisconsin. She is a forty-year-old Caucasian female with ten years of teaching experience and thirty-eight graduate credits. The interview with Ms. Wallace took place at a coffee shop in the city where she teaches.

Ms. Wallace was born in Germany and moved to the United States after completing her undergraduate degree in teaching in Germany. Upon moving to the United States, she completed a master's degree program at a public Midwestern university, which allowed her to receive her teaching license in the United States. She has enjoyed teaching in the United States ever since.

Essentially, Ms. Wallace had completed two pre-service teacher education programs, one at the undergraduate level in Germany and one at the graduate level in the United States. Both should be considered pre-service because they occurred prior to her first year of teaching. However, when speaking to Ms. Wallace during the interview, it was clear that she considered her undergraduate education in Germany her pre-service teacher education.

Like Ms. Foster, Ms. Wallace was satisfied with her pre-service teacher education experience and willing to become involved in her local pre-service teacher education program. In the survey, Ms. Wallace rated her pre-service teacher education experience as very good (a four on a five point scale). She reported that her pre-service teacher education experience was mostly relevant (a four on a five point scale) and somewhat prepared (a three on a five point scale) her for her first year of teaching. She clarified in the interview that she used her pre-service teacher education in Germany to answer these questions.

The only item for which she felt unprepared was "school policies." Because of the cultural differences between German and American schools and society, it is quite understandable that school policies would be foreign to Ms. Wallace. The politics and norms of schools and school teachers would have certainly been quite different in Germany, where she completed her elementary and secondary education. She did not have as much experience in American schools or American society as other first year teachers. This would have likely made working with students, colleagues, administrators, and parents much more challenging. In the interview, Ms. Wallace described her pre-service teacher education experience:

> It's something I did in Germany. I did, and it was a transitional time because it was coming from East Germany to West Germany. You know, we had to adapt the system. I did my university degree in four years. I was trained in German and English and some education classes also, and did my field experience during this time, you know, was already phased into teaching. And then the wall came down and they adopted the West German system and we had to do the two year internship . . . And the internship was really good too; it was educational. Once a week, we met on Mondays to do education classes to discuss what we have experienced. In retrospect, I think they were good classes. While I was taking them, I often felt like, you know, they weren't really satisfactory. But in retrospect, I think I did learn a lot: how to assess, how to design papers, tests, you know, things like this. I really feel that it really did help me. However, in coming to the United States, I had to relearn everything again because it was a little bit different than in Germany.

On the survey, Ms. Wallace marked no opinion to the questions on current pre-service teacher education. During the interview, she explained that she was not familiar with the American system of pre-service teacher education. I asked Ms. Wallace if her experience as a cooperating teacher to four student teachers in recent years had provided any insights into pre-service teacher education in the United States. She did note that "the difficulties that they maybe had was classroom management or feeling comfortable, you know presenting who you are in front of the kids."

Ms. Wallace did not fault the pre-service teacher education program for these deficiencies, however. She explained, "This is more something that you will gain through experience." Later in the interview, she did suggest that her student teachers would have benefited from more field experience.

Ms. Wallace believed that the content courses and field experiences were the most valuable part of her pre-service preparation in Germany. Based on her undergraduate experiences in Germany and her classroom teaching experience in the United States, she recommended that pre-service teacher education in the United States should focus more on these two areas. She felt quite strongly about both.

Ms. Wallace recommended that pre-service teachers "should take a lot of content area classes first and maybe fewer education classes." She believed that a deep knowledge, understanding, and passion for the content area were essential for any teacher to be effective, especially new teachers. Ms. Wallace explained, "I really think that you should be an expert in your subject. Before you become a good teacher, you have to know what you are teaching." The content courses were also her favorite part of her undergraduate experience. She said that she "really, really enjoyed" the courses in her content area, German and English.

Ms. Wallace also believed that education courses should be content specific, rather than generalized to include all education majors. Her pre-service teacher education courses in Germany were specific to her content area. "We were only foreign language . . . so yes we were divided by content area."

By contrast, most of the education courses Ms. Wallace had completed in her master's degree program in the United States included all grade levels and content areas. "There were elementary school teachers . . . Then, I have to listen to all the experiences that don't pertain to me, that's too much for me." She explained, "I would rather focus on my subject area." Ms. Wallace believed that having education courses that were content specific, in both pre-service and in-service teacher education, was "more valuable for me, personally."

Ms. Wallace also believed it was very important for veteran teachers to continue to be engaged in professional development to expand their knowledge of their content area. She believed that in-service teacher education should offer teachers more professional development opportunities in their content area. She said, "I would like to know, for example, new trends in European literature . . . then I would also like to know how to teach that." Wallace even suggested that professional development courses in the content area be required for continuing education and licensure. She argued, "You should prove that you have continued with your education in your content area."

Ms. Wallace did not speak highly of the in-service days at her school because it was too generalized and did not address any issues or strategies specific to her content area. In her opinion, in-service teacher education and professional development opportunities in the United States focused too much on pedagogy. While she appreciated being able to "learn new things, [and] new strategies," she was concerned about the lack of attention paid to one's content area. In her experience, all teachers were lumped together in teacher in-services and graduate education courses. She wanted more professional development opportunities specific to her content area. She explained:

> I'm a German teacher. I would love to be able to do something with German or with literature. You know, I'm a foreign language teacher so I would like to do something with the Spanish teacher, with the French teacher, in literature. Modern trends in European literature, for example, would be one thing that, you know, I would be interested in.

Ms. Wallace recommended that pre-service teachers should complete two years (or four semesters) of student teaching, as she had done. She believed that one semester of student teaching in pre-service teacher education was inadequate. Most pre-service teacher education programs in the United States require just one semester of student teaching. In Germany, she had completed two years of student teaching, but the field experience

actually began before that in the second year of her undergraduate program. At the beginning of the second year, the pre-service teachers were
required to be in the classroom once per week.

In the interview, Ms. Wallace explained, "We had to go into the classroom and teach part of a class, just like 15 minutes or so . . . do the intro-
duction, do the exercise, do the practice." Based on her own experience,
she concluded, "The early field experience is definitely something that did
help." In the United States, she had worked with four student teachers and
she felt the student teaching semester was "very overwhelming because
they have not had any experience." "They're scared," she said. According
to Ms. Wallace, "When you phase them in [gradually], they have a better
chance to feel more comfortable once they start the student teaching, so
I like that."

Ms. Wallace also believed that elementary and secondary teachers
should probably (a four on a five point scale) be more involved and influential in pre-service teacher education. When asked on the survey if she
would be willing to meet with faculty members from a university, she said
probably yes (a four on a five point scale). Other than the supervisors of
her student teachers, she had never met with any teacher educators from
her local university to discuss pre-service teacher education.

Ms. Wallace believed that regular meetings between teachers and
teacher educators would be quite beneficial (a four on a five point scale).
During the interview, she explained, "The professor needs the connection
to the school and the teacher needs the connection to the university." She
continued, "If the professors know what teachers want in the community
or in the school community, they can prepare them." She also believed
that better prepared pre-service teachers would then benefit the schools,
where they may someday teach. She said, "We would like to have good
teachers that come to our schools and we would like for them to be trained
well so you have to communicate often."

On the survey, Ms. Wallace indicated that she would definitely (a five
on a five point scale) be willing to guest teach at a university education
course for a day. She also reported that she would probably (a four on a
five point scale) be willing to teach part time. During the interview, she
explained that she had marked probably because she didn't know if she
would have the time to do it in her busy schedule. She also admitted that
she might be nervous about it. "I haven't taught a university class yet."

Despite these apparent challenges, Ms. Wallace became excited as she talked about the possibility of spending some time working with pre-service teachers at a local university. She said, "I would really like to, I mean, I wouldn't mind at all teaching a class in the summer, for example." Ms. Wallace thought that she had a lot of experiences, strategies, and resources that she could share that would benefit pre-service teachers, especially foreign language teachers. She stated, "I feel that if they had the opportunity to work with the students at the university level before they start their student teaching, for example, I think the kids, the students, would benefit from that a lot."

She also specified that "a math teacher should work with math students" and "history should work with history students." She continued by saying, "I don't know how to necessarily teach history, but I know how to teach foreign language." She explained that as a foreign language teacher, she would be able to share a variety of different ways to "introduce vocabulary in a foreign language." In other words, she believed that practicing teachers could help pre-service teachers develop pre-service teachers' pedagogical content knowledge and skills in the subjects they teach.

The interview with Ms. Wallace revolved around two major themes: content preparation and field experience. First, she believed quite strongly that pre-service teachers must be better prepared in their content area. She recommended that pre-service teachers complete more content area courses and fewer education courses. Ms. Wallace spoke much more positively, in general, about content courses than education courses. In education courses, she "always felt like gosh why do I need to know [that]." Conversely, she stated, "I really, really enjoyed my content area classes." She also believed that the education courses they do complete should be specific to their content area, as they were in Germany.

The second major theme that repeated itself through our conversation was that pre-service teachers need more field experience. She based this recommendation on her own experience as an undergraduate education major in Germany. In her pre-service preparation, she completed a two year student teaching experience. She had also been in the classroom once a week during the year before her student teaching experience. Her experience working with student teachers as a cooperating teacher in the United States has only confirmed her position. She felt strongly that her student teachers were overwhelmed because they hadn't spent enough time in the classroom.

Ms. Wallace believed that many of the abilities and skills needed by pre-service teachers were best learned through field experience. She cited classroom management and being comfortable in front of the class as examples. She believed that these skills were quite difficult to teach in the university classroom. She did recall the use of "scenarios" in her pre-service training in Germany. She believed this was the most effective university-based approach to learning these skills.

She also believed that pre-service teachers needed more pre-student teaching field experiences. She stated, "In my opinion, what they should do with student teachers is they should phase them in." In her opinion, the experience of "standing in front of a classroom" in the pre-student teaching field experiences helps the student teacher "feel more comfortable once they start the student teaching."

MEET MR. CLARK: A FIFTH GRADE TEACHER

Mr. Clark teaches reading, spelling, English, and social studies to fifth grade students at a small rural Wisconsin middle school. He is a fifty-year-old Caucasian male with twenty-four years of teaching experience and twenty-eight graduate credits. The interview with Mr. Clark took place at a fast food restaurant in the city where he lives and teaches. From the moment the interview began, it was clear that Mr. Clark was passionate about teaching and eager to share his ideas on pre-service teacher education.

Like Ms. Foster and Ms. Wallace, Mr. Clark was generally satisfied with his own pre-service teacher education experience. In the survey, Mr. Clark rated his own pre-service teacher education experience as very good (a four on a five point scale). He had attended a traditional undergraduate pre-service teacher education program at a public Midwestern university, where he completed bachelor's degrees in elementary and special education.

In the interview, Mr. Clark credited his professors with providing him with a relevant and valuable pre-service experience. He said, "Some of the profs I had, I think were pretty good." He later explained how one professor was particularly helpful as Mr. Clark returned to the university after being in the Air Force for four years. At the same time, Mr. Clark was also quick to point out that not all professors were that helpful or effective. "I had profs that I thought were a waste of time."

Mr. Clark also believed that the most effective professors modeled effective teaching for the pre-service teachers. He mentioned that he learned a lot about teaching from "watching the profs." He described one education professor who was "just a sweet lady, but she let the kids [pre-service teachers] run over her." In another education course, the professor was "just a little short thing, heart problems and all this kind of stuff, but she had total control of the class." He concluded, "Just watching those two ladies teach, I learned a lot about how to keep structure in a classroom, how to keep discipline in a classroom."

Overall, Mr. Clark believed his pre-service teacher education experience was mostly relevant (a four on a five point scale) and he felt mostly prepared (a four on a five point scale) for his first year of teaching. The only thing he reported feeling unprepared for was "cheating." In the interview, Mr. Clark also complained about the "long, long, long, long" lesson plans that were required during his pre-service experience.

According to the survey, Mr. Clark was also mostly satisfied (a four on a five point scale) with current pre-service teacher education. He explained that he based his evaluation mostly on the quality of student teachers that had worked in his building. Although he had never been a cooperating teacher himself, he was quite familiar with the student teachers in his building. "They seem to be pretty well prepared," he commented.

Although most of the student teachers did alright, their level of preparation seemed to vary quite dramatically, according to Mr. Clark. As he had done with his professors, Mr. Clark proceeded to contrast two student teachers who had worked at his school, as if to show that the quality varied. One student teacher was teaching a fifth grade social studies unit and "didn't have an accurate view of the constitution." Later, Mr. Clark had another student teacher and "he knew way more."

Mr. Clark believed that teachers and their ideas should probably (a four on a five point scale) be more involved in pre-service teacher education. In the interview, he explained that he thought teachers should have "some sort of input." He believed that teachers could provide teacher educators with "realistic feedback from somebody in the trenches versus somebody that hasn't done it for a while."

However, unlike Ms. Foster and Ms. Wallace, Mr. Clark was unwilling to become involved in pre-service teacher education. When asked if he was willing to meet with university faculty members, guest teach, or teach part-time, Mr. Clark responded probably not (a two on a five point scale) for all four questions. He was slightly more open to teaching full-time for one year at the university, where he replied maybe (a three on a five point scale).

In the interview, he explained that he was not interested in becoming involved in pre-service teacher education because he is toward the end of his career and is not a cooperating teacher. He was also unsure if he "could really make a difference." After twenty-eight years in education, he had become somewhat skeptical of new reforms or trends in education.

The primary theme of the interview with Mr. Clark was his belief in realistic preparation. He emphasized that pre-service teacher education should "make them aware of what it's really going to be like." In his view, new teachers often feel a sense of "discouragement, jeez, this isn't what I thought, you know." Mr. Clark identified positive and negative experiences in his own pre-service preparation to support his views. He identified "mock teacher conferences" as a realistic experience that he enjoyed and endorsed. According to Mr. Clark, the professor was "preparing us for things that are real in life that I would have never have thought about."

On the other hand, Mr. Clark identified "detailed lesson plans" as an unrealistic experience. Referring to the lesson plans he wrote in college, Mr. Clark said, "You had to have every part of that just perfect." He added, "There's so many other things that maybe you could be teaching instead."

Due to his belief in the importance of realistic preparation, Mr. Clark supported the increased involvement of practicing teachers in pre-service teacher education. Even though he was not very willing to become involved himself, he believed that practicing teachers would be able to "share real life experiences." According to Clark, the pre-service teachers would then have a better understanding of "the things you're going to run into."

Mr. Clark also supported requiring teacher educators to have K–12 classroom experience for the reason that it might result in more realistic preparation. In addition, Clark felt that teacher educators should "go back every so often on their sabbaticals." In his view, "Even after you've done it, you get away from it and you start becoming more and more idealistic or unrealistic."

The other themes that emerged from the interview with Mr. Clark, classroom management and group psychology, were also very much related to realistic preparation. Mr. Clark felt that addressing the issue of classroom management was very important and he was particularly concerned with "how to deal with that personality of a mob, a larger group." He believed that pre-service teachers were not very well prepared to deal with a large group of students. He explained how one particular group of students caused trouble for a long-term substitute at their school, who had just recently graduated.

> One thing I guess I've learned over the years is you can have a bunch of nice kids in a classroom, but when you get a mass of people together. There's a psychology there; there's a group personality that can take on a multiple of faces and it can be a nasty or a nice personality. . . . And you get those kids individually, they're pretty nice kids, but when they get in that group, they'll devour you. They'll just get you going, see what they can do to you, see if they can run you out, and I see that happening with one of our teachers.

Unfortunately, Mr. Clark believed that the educational psychology course during his pre-service teacher education focused solely on the psychology and behavior of the individual. Because teachers often interact with students in group settings rather than alone, the attention to individual behavior was not very realistic. Rather, Mr. Clark felt that pre-service teachers needed to be better prepared to manage the behavior of the group more effectively.

MEET MR. COOK: A TECHNOLOGY EDUCATION TEACHER

Mr. Cook teaches technology education to seventh through twelfth grade students at a middle and high school in a small town in Wisconsin. He is a fifty-one-year-old Caucasian male with thirty years of teaching experience and over sixty-five graduate credits. The interview with Mr. Cook took place at a coffee shop near the town where he lived and taught.

Like the other teachers described in this chapter, Mr. Cook was satisfied with his own pre-service teacher education experience. In the survey, Mr. Cook rated his own pre-service teacher education experience as excellent (a five on a five point scale). He had attended a traditional undergraduate pre-service teacher education program at a public Midwestern university, and had later completed his master's degree in education. Mr. Cook reported that his pre-service teacher education experience was very relevant (a five on a five point scale) and that he felt mostly prepared (a four on a five point scale) for his first year of teaching. The only things he reported feeling unprepared for was the "paperwork" and "logistics of schools."

During the interview, Mr. Cook explained that one of his professors was very influential and had done an excellent job of preparing him to be a teacher. Mr. Cook recalled his experience:

> [He] really talked to us a long time about, we're going into a profession and we have to act professional, that you wear a tie to school and you dress up to school and you present yourself as a mister [rather than a first name], you know. I don't know that we do that that much anymore. I don't know that we try to relate to the kids on that level. I think we try to relate to kids on a different level, where we want to be more, I don't want to say friend, but more towards that.

Mr. Cook believed that he was "a lot more prepared for that kind of stuff," than pre-service teachers are today. He believed that his pre-service teacher education had prepared him well to be a teacher. He also mentioned that his professors had "prepared us in the subject matter." For these reasons, Mr. Cook had given his own pre-service preparation the highest possible mark.

Although he was very satisfied with his own pre-service preparation, Mr. Cook reported in the survey that he was mostly unsatisfied (a two on a five point scale) with current pre-service teacher education. All of the things that his professors had done well to prepare him to be a professional, he criticized current pre-service teacher education programs for lacking.

In his experience with student teachers at his school, he felt they completely lacked the skills to be professionals. He explained, "I've got student teachers that are coming wearing shorts, T-shirts, ripped jeans, not expecting kids to call them mister." Because of his frustration with their complete lack of professionalism, Mr. Cook had stopped taking student teachers from his local university.

He also felt that the student teachers could plan lessons, but were not able to respond to unexpected challenges. For example, he said, "What do you do when a computer goes down and you've got thirty kids waiting and one kid's computer isn't caught up?" He claimed that the student teachers were not prepared for these types of issues. "Some of the kids that I've had student teach, I don't see that they have any clue what to do, and I've usually got to step-in in a situation like that and try to get control." He believes that pre-service teachers are only prepared for "an ideal situation where everyone comes in wanting to learn, and that's not really the case."

Although Mr. Cook had many ideas to share, he was not very willing to get involved in pre-service teacher education himself. In the survey, when asked if teachers and their ideas should be more involved in pre-service teacher education, he replied no opinion. He also reported in the survey that he would probably not (a two on a five point scale) be willing to meet with university faculty or teach part-time at the university.

In the interview, Mr. Cook explained that one of the reasons he was unwilling to meet with teacher educators from the university was time. Mr. Cook commented, "I teach seven preps as it is." Teaching seven different classes each day, with minimal time during the day to prepare for each, has placed a large burden on Mr. Cook's time and leaves little time for other professional endeavors. In addition to teaching, Mr. Cook also coaches in the evening. This can sometimes keep him at the school until "eight, eight-thirty at night depending on what we've got and what season." This type of daily schedule would make meeting with anyone quite difficult.

Another reason Mr. Cook was generally unwilling to be involved was his perception that he was not respected by teacher educators. Mr. Cook mentioned that he was friends with some of the faculty members at the university in the technology related fields. However, he does not have the same relationship with faculty members in education. According to Mr. Cook, when he does "interact with some of the other ones from the education department, and I don't mean to pick on them specifically, I always get the feeling that they're looking down on me."

Mr. Cook believed that this lack of respect he felt was sometimes related to the subject area he teaches, technology education. He explained

that many other teachers and teacher educators have very negative perceptions of technology education students and teachers. He questioned this
common misconception, "Why is it that if you're in a vocation, you're
obviously aren't going to do anything else, you know?" "I went to college
. . . I'm not dumb," he said.

Because of this feeling of disrespect, Mr. Cook believed that regular
meetings between teachers and teacher educators would be only slightly
beneficial (a two on a five point scale). In his past interactions with faculty
members from the university, Mr. Cook also perceived a "feeling of aloof-
ness on both of our parts." He added, "I think we have to be welcomed
into the fold. . . . We don't want to go into someplace where we're not
wanted."

In other words, it might be important to build more trust and build
better relationships between teachers and teacher educators before these
types of meetings would generate any noticeable benefits. He commented,
"It would be nice to have somebody just say, yes, we want your opinion,
we want to work with you, and you're still valuable to us." He added,
"I would feel pretty good if I was a teacher and someone wanted me to
come back. I would feel like I was still valuable in a way." If he received
that type of invitation and validation, he indicated that he would consider
becoming more involved in pre-service teacher education, especially after
he retired from teaching.

In the survey, Mr. Cook did respond maybe (a three on a five point
scale) when asked if he would be willing to come to the university to guest
teach or speak in an education course. Similarly, he indicated he would
probably (a four on a five point scale) be willing to teach full-time for one
year in his local pre-service teacher education program. He also said he
would probably (a four on a five point scale) be willing to participate in a
teacher-faculty exchange in order to teach at the university for one year.
This would alleviate his concerns about trying to fit his involvement at the
university into his current secondary teaching schedule. If the scheduling
could be figured out, he was willing to at least consider it.

Mr. Cook suggested that he would be more likely to consider becoming
more involved after he retired. He noted, "Some of them [retiring teach-
ers] are not ready to give it up completely, but . . . they can't keep up that
schedule so they'll come back and do substitute teaching." He suggested
instead that those retiring teachers could "come back to this [teach at the

university] for a year or two, you know." He half-jokingly added, "Mc-Donald's has made it work for a long time where they bring in some older workers and the young kids learn how to work from them." He concluded, "It would be great to have some retired teachers coming in where they are working themselves out of a career, but training some new ones."

Although Mr. Cook thought it would be difficult for him personally, he did believe that involving teachers would be somewhat beneficial (a three on a five point scale). In the interview, he responded, "Absolutely . . . as long as everybody has an openness and willingness to learn, and I mean from both sides, my side, their side, everybody." Once again, it seemed that Mr. Cook was hesitant to think that his expertise and ideas would be respected by teacher educators. If everyone was open and willing to listen to one another, then Mr. Cook believed it could ultimately benefit pre-service teachers and their future students.

The issue of professionalism was a very prevalent theme in the interview with Mr. Cook. He believed that his own pre-service teacher education experience taught him "to act professional" and "to role model for kids" the behavior that should be expected from the students. Mr. Cook believed that professionalism had been lost in pre-service teacher education today as the attention shifted to other issues. "I don't know that you can allow for the lack of professionalism and that's where we've got a gap," he suggested. He continued, "It's like if you've got a plate that's only so big and you keep piling things on, something's going to fall off the other side and I think that's what's fallen off is the professionalism of what we do."

In fact, Mr. Cook remarked, "I've got to a point where I won't take student teachers." He shared a story of his experiences with one student teacher in particular who lacked professionalism. According to Mr. Cook, "There's always the allotment for being nervous in front of your class for the first time; you can always allow for that, but I don't know that you can allow for the lack of professionalism." Mr. Cook believed that teaching is "not just a job; this is kind of like a calling," and "they [student teachers] don't look at it as a calling."

Mr. Cook suggested that professionalism and commitment to the profession were more important than some of the other things being emphasized in pre-service teacher education, like the standards, standardized exams, and grade point averages. He suggested that "instead of weeding [pre-service teachers] out by grade points, that you weed out by people who are committed to their job."

Based on his experience, he believed that these pre-service teachers would ultimately be successful because of their commitment to education and their commitment to students. "They'd be a good teacher because they care about kids," he said. While Mr. Cook did not recommend specific strategies for teaching or measuring this type of professionalism and commitment to students, he felt it was vital to preparing effective teachers.

Like the interview with Mr. Clark, realistic preparation was another major theme during the interview with Mr. Cook and this led to several recommendations for improving pre-service teacher education. He believed that pre-service teachers needed more realistic preparation. He commented that pre-service teacher education was "too cerebral at the university level." He said, "Reality is high school and middle school and cerebral is what's being taught at the university." He felt that pre-service teachers were often presented with idealistic views of teaching. According to Mr. Cook, the university perpetuates an image of teaching where "everyone comes in wanting to learn and that's not really the case."

Instead, Mr. Cook suggested that pre-service teachers needed to be prepared for real situations. For example, although pre-service teachers learn to prepare lessons, Mr. Cook felt that pre-service teachers are not prepared for making "snap decisions" when things don't go as planned. "How do you handle those situations without having total chaos?" questioned Mr. Cook. Mr. Cook suggested that education courses should "set up exercises" to prepare student teachers for this type of quick decision-making.

Mr. Cook believed that requiring K–12 classroom experience for teacher educators would help make pre-service teacher education more realistic. He thought it would help teacher educators be less "cerebral." He commented that "it's important for them to see what the actual kid is like in class because theory and reality are two different things." Like Mr. Clark, Mr. Cook suggested that teacher educators be given "release time or semester sabbaticals" to spend more time in the K–12 classrooms. He explained, "I think once you're away from anything, you know, you're going to lose track of what's happening. I think that's what's happened with some of those [teacher educators]."

To provide more realistic preparation, Mr. Cook also suggested the amount of field experience in pre-service teacher education be increased and recommended two semesters of student teaching. He explained, "Instead of so much time with theory and that kind of stuff, I'd like to see people just out in the schools." He continued by saying, "I think the more time you can spend in front of a class or in a class observing, the better you're going to be prepared for it."

Although Mr. Cook believed that pre-service teacher education could be more realistic and better address the lack of professionalism, he did value the work of teacher educators. At the end of the interview, he concluded by saying, "I really believe universities are making their best effort. I think that they're doing an excellent job of preparing in all of the ways except the ones that I mentioned." As he neared the end of his teaching career, he expressed a concern for the future of his profession, especially if we allowed a profession to continue without a purposeful emphasis on professionalism.

8

Meet the Teachers Dissatisfied with Their Teacher Education Experience

The surveyed showed that nearly four out of five teachers (79 percent) rated their pre-service teacher education experience as good (31 percent), very good (30 percent), or excellent (18 percent). In the last chapter, you met four of these teachers. By comparison, only one in five teachers (21 percent) rated their pre-service teacher education experience as poor (5 percent) or fair (16 percent). Although there were far more teachers who are satisfied than dissatisfied with their pre-service experience, the number of teachers that are dissatisfied is still far too large.

What do these teachers think about pre-service teacher education? What are the views and beliefs that form the basis for their dissatisfaction? What do they recommend be changed to improve pre-service teacher education for the next generation of teachers?

In this chapter, you will meet four teachers who were all dissatisfied with their pre-service teacher education experience. Two were willing to become more involved in pre-service teacher education and two were not. Mr. Gray and Ms. Kraft were dissatisfied with their pre-service teacher education experience, but they both expressed a willingness to become involved. Mr. Ford and Ms. Nelson were dissatisfied with their pre-service teacher education experience and unwilling to become involved themselves. This chapter will share their stories, ideas, and beliefs.

MEET MR. GRAY: A HISTORY TEACHER

Mr. Gray teaches history, Spanish, political science, economics, and anthropology to ninth through twelfth grade students at a medium sized high school in Wisconsin. He is a forty-seven-year-old Caucasian male with twenty-two years of teaching experience and over sixty graduate credits. The interview with Mr. Gray took place in his high school classroom.

Mr. Gray was generally dissatisfied with his own pre-service teacher education experience, which he rated as fair (a two on a five point scale) on the survey. Like many of the teachers surveyed, he had attended a traditional undergraduate pre-service teacher education program at a public Midwestern university. On the survey, he described his pre-service teacher education experience as only somewhat relevant (a three on a five point scale) to the practice of teaching. In the end, he felt mostly unprepared (a two on a five point scale) for his first year of teaching.

Why did he feel so unsatisfied and unprepared by his pre-service preparation? Mr. Gray felt unprepared for "'real' teaching" as compared to the "'ideal' teaching" that was taught during his pre-service teacher education experience. He also identified "paperwork" as something that he had felt unprepared for as a first year teacher. He believed that pre-service teacher education would be much more effective "if the ideas matched the reals." Mr. Gray would return to this idea later in the interview.

Mr. Gray believed that too much time was spent on educational theory and abstractions. Although Mr. Gray believed that philosophies and theories of education should be taught, he suggested "those could be done a lot quicker." He suggested that less time be spent on other foundational ideas like educational psychology, the history of education, and multiculturalism. He reasoned that "most of us are not going to be education psychologists." In regard to multiculturalism, he argued, "you've already done that in your general ed." He pointed to courses in "world history" and "Indian literature" as examples. In his experience, Mr. Gray found these courses to be less helpful and less practical.

In addition, Mr. Gray explained that the lack of content preparation was another reason he was dissatisfied with his pre-service preparation. He stated, "I think most people at the junior high and high school aren't qualified in their fields to teach that subject, and that's why I think I rated that fair." On his survey, he had written, "How many teachers of history are historians?" Mr. Gray believed quite strongly that teachers needed to develop more content knowledge during pre-service teacher education, and this issue came up several other times during the interview.

Despite his overall negative perception of pre-service teacher education, Mr. Gray did share that one professor in particular had a very positive effect on his teaching career. This professor had taught him that "every kid in this room knows something about what we're going to talk about." Mr. Gray explained that this was now a very salient component to his own teaching philosophy. "Get them from where they are; get them to where you want them to be," he said. Mr. Gray testified, "I've noticed over the years that has worked."

On the survey, Mr. Gray responded no opinion to the questions on current pre-service teacher education. He explained that he was "unsure of the current practices." Mr. Gray had been a cooperating teacher for one student teacher; although he said he was somewhat informed about that particular program, he did not feel comfortable responding.

Although Mr. Gray had some sharp criticisms of his own pre-service teacher education experience, he did express a willingness to become involved in pre-service teacher education. On the survey, he indicated that he would probably (a four on a five point scale) be willing to meet with university faculty members to discus pre-service teacher education. Mr. Gray believed these meetings would be quite beneficial (a four on a five point scale).

In the interview, Mr. Gray explained that he could offer the university faculty a practical perspective on teaching and learning. He explained that it would especially help "that college professor who hasn't done a lot [of teaching in an elementary or middle school]." At the same time, Mr. Gray quickly clarified that he would prefer that teacher educators have more first-hand experience. "It would be better for a college professor to see that sometimes kids don't do their homework and sometimes kids don't care," he remarked.

Mr. Gray also indicated on the survey that he would probably be willing (a four on a five point scale) to guest teach or teach education courses part-time at the university. In fact, Mr. Gray had taught several courses in a master's degree program for teachers at a local private university. In his opinion, having elementary and secondary teachers as instructors in teacher education was a "good idea." Mr. Gray recommended involving cooperating teachers more as guest speakers or instructors in pre-service teacher education. He suggested that the "cooperating teacher should teach some of those Ed [education] classes."

Mr. Gray also liked the idea of co-teaching with a university faculty member, which he had never done before. He believed the two perspectives would complement one another. The university faculty member would bring a theoretical perspective and the K–12 teacher could explain "a number of ways those theories have been seen in a classroom." In this arrangement, he compared the teacher's role in co-teaching education courses to that of an assistant coach.

Three themes emerged from the interview with Mr. Gray: realistic preparation, field experience, and content preparation. These themes also identify issues that contributed to his overall poor rating of pre-service teacher education in the survey. First, Mr. Gray advocated for more realistic preparation and perceived pre-service teacher education as idealistic in nature. He claimed that too many teacher educators spent too much time on issues that did not have enough practical application to the classroom.

Mr. Gray believed that in many cases teacher educators "were talking about things that weren't really done in a classroom." He cited "individualized instruction" as one example. He explained, "If I have a class of 15, that's really neat. When you have 152 kids a day, you can't do that." He believed the educational system would need to be changed to provide students with the type of individualized instruction that is being advocated by teacher educators. "I just don't think there's enough teachers; I don't think there's enough money," for it to be practical.

Mr. Gray cited the formal lesson plans required in most education courses as another example of an unrealistic expectation for teachers. He also felt that a lesson plan should never be made for one day at a time, which is what was required of him during his pre-service experience. He argued, "In the real world, and that's what I mean that ideal versus real, a lesson on supply and demand, for example, may last a week and a half."

On the other hand, Mr. Gray had one education professor who required him to create quick lesson plans in "ten minutes." Mr. Gray believed that this type of lesson planning and preparation was much more realistic and useful. He believed the quick lesson plans better prepared him to be flexible as a teacher and change his lesson plans on short notice as needed.

This was the same professor that taught Mr. Gray that every student knew something about the topic he was teaching. From Mr. Gray's perspective, this professor was exceptional, and the exception to the typically idealistic preparation he had experienced during his pre-service teacher education.

Mr. Gray also believed that the unrealistic expectations and strategies taught in pre-service teacher education were partly responsible for the high rates of teacher attrition in the teaching profession. He was concerned about "the number of teachers that drop out that first couple of years because all of a sudden, they're thrown into that without any way to deal with it." He felt that teacher educators needed to be more realistic so that first year teachers would be better prepared for the challenges of the classroom.

Mr. Gray's belief in more realistic preparation also shaped his views on the importance of K–12 teaching experience for teacher educators and the potential benefits of more teacher involvement in pre-service teacher education. Gray believed it was important that "you've done the field that you claim you're going to be teaching." Gray hypothesized that teacher educators with K–12 experience would convey more realistic ideas and perspectives on teaching and learning and could potentially model lessons from their past teaching.

Finally, the need for more field experience was another theme that repeated itself throughout the interview with Mr. Gray. Mr. Gray recommended that pre-service teachers "should be doing a lot more observation of veteran teachers." He argued "that more experience in the classroom is more important than lectures." To Mr. Gray, it seemed very unrealistic to expect a pre-service teacher to learn to teach without more experiences in elementary and secondary classrooms. He explained, "I don't know how you teach that stuff unless you give experience. It's like if you're going to be a car mechanic, you can't just read about cars."

Mr. Gray shared his experience of observing at an elementary school. It had helped him when he got his first job at a middle school. Referring to his own pre-service teacher education experience, he said, "We had to observe classes that we were never going to teach." Gray believed that pre-service teachers needed more field experience and opportunities to observe multiple teachers at multiple grade levels. He recommended two semesters of student teaching. Mr. Gray believed that pre-service teachers needed to "get in there and get your hands dirty." He reasoned that the field experience was more valuable than "just sitting in class memorizing the philosophy of, you know, education."

The final theme that emerged from the interview was Mr. Gray's belief that middle school and high school teachers needed more content preparation. This was one of the reasons Mr. Gray had rated his pre-service preparation so poorly in the first place. He mentioned the lack of content preparation at the beginning of the interview and returned to this issue several times later in the interview. In his discipline, Mr. Gray used the example of economics where just nine credits of college economics could certify a social studies teacher to teach economics.

Mr. Gray believed that "most people at the junior high and high school aren't qualified in their fields to teach that subject." He stated that "if you're going to be a chemistry teacher, you should be a chemist." Mr. Gray recommended that middle and high school teachers should have at least a college minor in the fields they teach, and preferably a college major. He concluded, "I don't think they should be allowed to teach a course unless they have a minor and we're giving them more classroom experience."

MEET MS. KRAFT: A HISTORY TEACHER

Ms. Kraft teaches ninth through twelfth grade social studies at a fairly large high school in Wisconsin. She is a thirty-five-year-old Caucasian female with twelve years of teaching experience and thirty-nine graduate credits. She left the teaching profession in the spring semester, after the survey and before the interview was conducted. The interview with Ms. Kraft took place at a coffee shop near her home.

Like Mr. Gray, Ms. Kraft was dissatisfied with her pre-service teacher education experience, but still willing to become involved. In the survey, Ms. Kraft rated her own pre-service teacher education experience as good (a three on a five point scale). She had completed her bachelor's degree as a history and psychology double major before returning to school to complete her pre-service teacher education program as an undergraduate at a public Midwestern university.

She later completed her master's degree in educational technology. She reported that her pre-service teacher education experience was somewhat relevant (a three on a five point scale) and that she felt somewhat prepared (a three on a five point scale). She recalled feeling unprepared for "classroom management" and "time management" during her first year of teaching.

In the interview, Ms. Kraft explained that her pre-service teacher education program taught "a lot of content and not a lot of methodology and there's no practicum whatsoever." She felt like she needed more knowledge and applications of teaching methods. She was especially adamant that she did not have enough opportunities to apply her knowledge and develop her skills in front of real students. Ms. Kraft did clarify that she did have the opportunity to spend time in a classroom during field experiences. However, she did not have the opportunity to practice her teaching skills during those field experiences. She explained, "You can go in and observe, but observing isn't the same as doing . . . so that's why I rated it as good."

Ms. Kraft emphasized that teaching involved working with kids and that teachers needed to develop strong interpersonal skills to be prepared for their first year of teaching.

> There's a saying that says kids don't care what you know until they know you care, and what the college teaches you is what you know. They don't teach you or let you practice how to care so that's why I said it was good. I mean I got the content I needed, but I didn't get any of the practical stuff that I needed.

Ms. Kraft believed that her pre-service teacher education had been lacking in the practical strategies she needed to be better prepared as a pre-service teacher. She also believed that she needed more opportunities to practice these strategies during field experiences. Finally, Ms. Kraft also criticized her education professors for not modeling best practices. She said, "They don't practice what they preach." For example, she explained, "They don't practice multiple intelligences . . . I mean it was primarily lecture and that's because you have large classes."

For many of the same reasons, Ms. Kraft reported that she was mostly dissatisfied (a two on a five point scale) with current pre-service teacher education. She also based her evaluation of current pre-service teacher education on her experiences with student teachers. Ms. Kraft had

supervised six student teachers during her twelve years of teaching experience. She concluded from these experiences that "too little focuses
on reality." She added, "Everything is theory and that's not reality." Ms.
Kraft believed that there was a significant gap (a four on a five point
scale) between what is taught in current pre-service teacher education and
what is practiced in secondary classrooms.

In the interview, Ms. Kraft explained that her student teachers were
lacking in preparation for managing the classroom and student behavior.
She stated, "They struggle with the hands-on; they struggle with the discipline." She complained, "There's zero on behavioral control; there's zero
classroom discipline." Ms. Kraft suggested, "Those are issues that should
be addressed before student teaching."

Related to their ability to manage the classroom, Ms. Kraft believed
that her student teachers had not spent enough time in the classroom prior
to student teaching. She believed that learning to manage the classroom
and discipline students required experience, far more experience than
what was currently allotted in most pre-service teacher education programs. Ms. Kraft recommended "more of the prestudent teaching kind of
thing so that when you get to student teaching, there's a significant difference in the training."

Despite her dissatisfaction with pre-service teacher education, Ms. Kraft
was willing to become involved in pre-service teacher education. On the
survey, she reported that she would definitely (a five on a five point scale)
be willing to meet with teacher educators to discuss pre-service teacher
education, and it was something that she had done before. In the interview,
she explained that it would help pre-service teacher education to be more
practical and lead to "better teachers, more confident teachers."

On the survey, Ms. Kraft also reported that she would maybe (a three
on a scale of five) teach part-time, probably (a four on a scale of five)
guest teach for a day, and definitely (five on a scale of five) teach full-time
for a year. In the interview, she explained that teaching part-time would be
most difficult because it is difficult to get "release from the teaching day."
She said, "A good teacher doesn't [just] work from 7 to 3." She suggested,
"To make it happen, you'd have to find a good way to compensate time,
not so much money, but time."

Because of the time constraints, she believed that teaching full-time at
the university for one year was a much more practical idea. If it could be
worked out, Ms. Kraft would love to teach at the university level. "That

would be awesome because it's fun and the other thing is you get to deal with adults on a different level; they might only be a year or two older than high school, but they're adults on a different level."

The two themes that emerged from the interview with Ms. Kraft were realistic preparation and field experience. Reflecting on her own pre-service teacher education experience, she said, "I got the content I needed, but I didn't get any of the practical stuff that I needed." She criticized teacher educators for being overly theoretical. "If everything the college teaches could be put into play, it would be awesome, but that's not the reality," she explained.

In her view, the teaching methods that were taught in pre-service teacher education were difficult to implement in a real classroom. She remarked, "The reality is that everything that's taught is methodology and it's great in theory." She explained that the lack of resources, computers, student motivation, preparation time, and time to collaborate with colleagues in real schools were the major obstacles to implementing the strategies taught in her pre-service education experience. In her view, it was impossible to plan, teach, and assess in the ways she learned at the university, because of these constraints.

Like Mr. Clark, Ms. Kraft believed that the formal lesson plans taught in pre-service teacher education were very unrealistic. She commented, "I came out of college writing beautiful lesson plans and you know how long they lasted?" Again, the lack of preparation time was the reason she identified for not being able to write formal lesson plans once she began teaching. She explained, "You think you're going to get something done in 45 minutes and then the announcements come on and then a student needs to go to the bathroom and now you have 34 minutes."

On the other hand, she believed that more time should be devoted to classroom management and discipline strategies. According to Ms. Kraft, "There's zero on classroom management and the number one and two things that you have to have when you're coming into a classroom are behavior control and classroom discipline." She believed that preparation in classroom management was particularly important for student teachers and new teachers. According to Kraft, "They struggle with the discipline . . . wanting to bend over backwards to help a kid and not realizing that there's lines."

She also commented that teacher educators "don't practice what they preach," but instead "primarily lecture." In order to provide more realistic preparation, she believed that teacher educators should be required to have K–12 experience and assumed that most currently do not. She stated, "They might have master degrees and Ph.D.'s, but they don't have the experience."

Ms. Kraft compared learning to teach to learning to build a house, and explained, "It's like . . . telling somebody you're going to build a house and here's a book that tells you how." She believed that teacher educators needed to convey more than book knowledge. They needed to teach preservice teachers how that knowledge could be applied with real kids in real classrooms. In her opinion, this required that teacher educators have experience in K–12 classrooms.

The other theme that emerged from the interview with Ms. Kraft was the need for more field experience. This was closely related to the perceived need for more realistic or practical preparation. In essence, the field experience would reinforce and apply what was learned in the university classroom, in much more practical ways.

Although Ms. Kraft recommended more field experiences, she recommended only one semester of student teaching. She believed "you're going to get pretty much everything in a whole semester that you're going to get in a whole year." She was also very concerned about the tuition cost for an additional semester of student teaching. Rather than lengthen the student teaching experience, Ms. Kraft strongly advocated for "more of the prestudent teaching."

Ms. Kraft recommended that pre-student teaching occur in every year of the preparation program. "I think teaching should be more hands-on all the way through the program . . . Year one through year four, you're in the room, you're in the classroom, you're involved, [and] you're doing different things." Ms. Kraft also recommended that student teachers "should have experience at every [grade] level," even at grade levels they would never teach. She believed this would better prepare pre-service teachers to work in schools, and place their role in the school system into the proper context.

MEET MR. FORD: A HISTORY TEACHER

Mr. Ford teaches U.S. history and economics to tenth and eleventh grade students at a medium sized high school in Wisconsin. He is a twenty-nine-year-old Caucasian male with three years of teaching experience and nine graduate credits. The interview with Mr. Ford took place at a coffee shop near the city where he lives and teaches.

Like Mr. Gray and Ms. Kraft, Mr. Ford was generally dissatisfied with his pre-service teacher education experience. He had attended a traditional undergraduate pre-service teacher education program at a public Midwestern university. In the survey, Mr. Ford rated his pre-service teacher education experience as fair (a two on a five point scale). He believed it was only somewhat relevant (a three on a five point scale) and left him feeling mostly unprepared (a two on a five point scale) for his first year of teaching.

In particular, Mr. Ford reported being unprepared for classroom management. He wrote, "It is a joke that this is not discussed in ed [education] programs. It should be a class itself." In truth, most pre-service teacher education programs do have a course in classroom management. Mr. Ford either attended a program that did not include one or took one and completely forgot about it. Either way, his preparation for managing the classroom was completely lacking. Even for those programs that included an effective classroom management course, this remains an area that needs more attention, as discussed in the previous chapters.

In the interview, Mr. Ford stated emphatically, "I definitely, I wasn't ready." He said, "Looking back now I almost feel sorry for the kids that had them their first year. You know, I think it was that bad." He explained, "Classroom management was my biggest flaw, and I would say secondarily it would be just organization skills and being prepared." He said, "It wasn't really discussed."

His professors seemed to promote the idea that "if you plan well enough, you don't have to worry about it." He said about the students, "They're bringing so much baggage into the classroom, you don't know what's going on on a daily basis in their lives." He said, "They come into the classroom, and they're dead tired, and they're not doing anything, and then they're telling everybody about it, you know."

While he believed that planning could alleviate some potential classroom management issues, it was not enough. He believed a course that focused on motivating students and managing student behavior more effectively was something that he was missing in his pre-service preparation. He concluded, "Having a class like that, I think, would be absolutely invaluable."

The quality of the professors was another reason he was dissatisfied with his pre-service teacher education experience and felt unprepared for his first year of teaching. He discussed this during the interview. Mr. Ford shared, "I was very disappointed with my experience there, with teacher education." He explained, "A lot of the professors that were there when I was there, they're now gone, so maybe that says something." He described one professor as a "bit of a flake." She focused largely on the "philosophy of education," rather than the more practical concerns that Mr. Ford valued. He also felt that many of the other professors focused too much on the elementary level, which was not as relevant for Mr. Ford as a secondary teacher.

Like other teachers, Mr. Ford did report having one professor in particular that had a positive effect on his pre-service preparation. Mr. Ford commented, "The one that I liked had classroom experience. The ones that I didn't, as far as I know of, I don't know if they had any real classroom experience." He later added, "If you could maybe go and get your Ph.D. in education without ever having taught, if it were like that, I would have a real problem with that." Mr. Ford strongly valued and respected the expertise of this one professor because of his classroom experience.

Mr. Ford was also dissatisfied with current pre-service teacher education, for many of the same reasons. Mr. Ford believed that pre-service teacher education was "not realistic enough," and pre-service teachers were not prepared for the classroom. Once again, Mr. Ford returned to the need for pre-service teachers to be better prepared for classroom management issues. "I get so worked up about this classroom management thing," he said.

He believed there was a significant gap (a four on a five point scale) between what is taught in pre-service teacher education and what is experienced in elementary and secondary classrooms. To remedy this lack of realistic preparation, Mr. Ford recommended that pre-service teachers needed "more (paid) time as a student teacher." He recommended that all pre-service programs should require two semesters of student teaching. Interestingly, he also recommended that student teachers should be paid, "even if minimum wage," for their services in the school.

Despite his overall dissatisfaction with pre-service teacher education, Mr. Ford spoke very highly of his student teaching experience and his cooperating teachers. "I had a great student teaching experience," he said. He described his cooperating teachers as "supportive" and very good at providing "constructive feedback regularly." Based on his experience, he concluded, "It would have been nice [to have] another semester to keep working there."

When asked if practicing teachers and their ideas should be more involved in pre-service teacher education, Mr. Ford responded no opinion on the survey. In the interview, it was clear that he had not understood the question. He thought the question was about involving more teachers in working with student teachers. He explained that some of his colleagues should not be working with student teachers.

When asked if teachers should be more involved in all aspects of pre-service teacher education, including the university-based coursework, he changed his response. He responded, "I think that would be fantastic." He explained that teachers could bring "the practical classroom experience of here's what I do in a high school classroom and this worked and this doesn't work for me." He believed that practicing teachers would be able to help pre-service teachers to select, use, and create curriculum and develop strategies for dealing with particular classroom management issues.

In the survey, Mr. Ford indicated that he was reluctant to get involved himself. When asked if he would be willing to meet with university faculty members, guest teach or speak in an education course, or teach full-time for one year at the university, he responded maybe (a three on a five point scale). Although he believed that meetings or teaching an education course would be somewhat beneficial (a three on a five point scale), he explained that his schedule would not allow it.

Mr. Ford was a class advisor, soccer coach, and lead negotiator for the union. He and his wife were also expecting a new baby. He said, "I would like to do it, but the reality of it, I'm not sure I could pull if off." In fact, Mr. Ford did mention that he had considered "going back and working towards a Ph.D. someday." He said, "I would love to teach at the university level."

There were two major themes that emerged during the interview with Mr. Ford. The first theme was the quality of the education professors. Mr. Ford experienced one good professor during his pre-service preparation. He remarked, "There was one that was fantastic and the rest I could have done without." In regards to the other education professors, he said, "I was really disappointed with them, and I just mean, I mean, they were poor teachers."

Mr. Ford believed that most of his education professors did not model effective teaching practices or the methods they recommended to their students. Ford described the predominant teaching method used in education courses as a "classic classroom lecture." He characterized the lack of modeling in pre-service teacher education as "complete hypocrisy." He said, "Holding the professors to model what they are teaching would be kind of a base, a minimum, a bare minimum." His negative perception of his education professors had a very negative effect on his view of pre-service teacher education.

The second major theme of the interview with Mr. Ford was classroom management. He felt strongly that classroom management was a weakness of pre-service teacher education. He stated that classroom management "was never discussed" and this was his "biggest, biggest issue" with pre-service teacher education.

Mr. Ford simply felt unprepared to teach in his first year of teaching, especially in the area of classroom management. He commented, "Classroom management was definitely my biggest flaw." He later added, "Like I said, I had no clue; I had no clue what to do to manage a classroom." This feeling of being unprepared for the task of managing the students, classroom space, and activities in the classroom likely shaped his other views on pre-service teacher education quite negatively.

His dissatisfaction with the professors and the lack of classroom management preparation explain his low rating of pre-service teacher education. These strongly held beliefs also help to explain many of his other views expressed in both the survey and interview. Mr. Ford believed strongly that there was a significant gap between the university and schools.

To address this gap, Mr. Ford had several recommendations. First, he recommended that schools and universities should form professional development school partnerships. According to Mr. Ford, this might bring a more practical perspective to teacher preparation. Second, he believed that someone should not be able to earn a Ph.D. in education without K–12 experience. Based on his own experience, Mr. Ford felt that some of his education professors were not qualified or effective as teacher educators. If they had been elementary or secondary teachers first, Mr. Ford believed that would be able to better prepare pre-service teachers for the classroom.

Finally, Mr. Ford recommended that pre-service teachers should complete two semesters of student teaching. He believed that teachers needed to learn about teaching and learning in a more practical context. During the field experiences, pre-service teachers would be able to observe and apply what they are learning at the university. In particular, Mr. Ford believed that students needed to be in the classroom to learn important classroom management strategies and techniques. The poor quality of education professors and a lack of preparation in classroom management were issues that Mr. Ford believed needed to be addressed.

MEET MS. NELSON: A SCIENCE TEACHER

Ms. Nelson teaches earth science to ninth through twelfth grade students at a large high school in Wisconsin. She is a thirty-four-year-old Caucasian female with six years of teaching experience and twenty-four graduate credits. The interview with Ms. Nelson took place at her home.

Like Mr. Ford, Ms. Nelson was dissatisfied with pre-service teacher education and unwilling to become involved. She had attended a traditional undergraduate pre-service teacher education program at a public Midwestern university. In the survey, Ms. Nelson rated her pre-service teacher education experience as fair (a two on a five point scale). She reported that her experience was somewhat relevant (a three on a five point scale) to the practice of teaching and that she felt somewhat prepared (a three on a five point scale) for her first year of teaching. The only thing for which she felt completely unprepared was "dealing with parents."

In the interview, Ms. Nelson also added classroom management as something she felt unprepared to address as a first year teacher. She explained, "I can teach my science stuff, but it's all that other stuff. It's the classroom management. It's dealing with the parents. It's the dealing with the administration." She admitted, even in her sixth year of teaching, "That's still my biggest problem." She added, "If I could just stay within my room and never have to deal with anything outside of my room, it's a perfect job."

Ms. Nelson did report that she felt prepared to teach her subject area of science. She said, "The science methods courses were of the most benefit to me." She spoke very highly of the two professors who taught the science methods courses. She also explained that they "were science teachers at one point," before becoming teacher educators. According to

Ms. Nelson, these two professors, and the two university teaching methods courses they taught, had an enormous influence on her beliefs about teaching science and her future practice as a science teacher.

> Everything was hands-on, minds-on, and I carried that over into [my teaching], you now. I don't use the book as much and everything else, so that was the most beneficial to me because it gave me ideas. I wasn't taught science that way. I was taught you had the book, you read the section, you do the questions at the end, so it was nice to have that to know that there are other ways to go about teaching kids the science.

Ms. Nelson was not very willing to become involved in pre-service teacher education. She indicated that she would maybe (a three on a five point scale) be willing to meet with university faculty members to discuss teacher education, maybe be willing to guest teach an education course for one day, and maybe be willing to teach full-time for one year at the university. Ms. Nelson explained that she was expecting another baby, and did not have a lot of time after school to become involved in her local pre-service teacher education program. She also explained, "I don't feel like seven years [is enough or] that my information was going to be useful."

Although she was not very willing to become involved herself, Ms. Nelson believed that teachers should probably (a four on a five point scale) be more involved in pre-service teacher education. In the interview, she recommended that veteran teachers should be more involved in pre-service teacher education programs and could make a valuable contribution. Ms. Nelson believed that veteran elementary and secondary teachers should be "taking their experience and sharing it with people that're just getting into the field." She admitted that she still goes to the veteran teachers in her building when she has a question or needs help with something. "Those are the ones I go to all the time," she said.

Ms. Nelson believed that involving veteran teachers in regular meetings with teacher educators or teaching education courses would be somewhat beneficial (a three on a five point scale). She felt that these teachers might be able to share more about what teaching is really like in the field, including some of the most challenging aspects of the job.

She believed that this might help prepare some pre-service teachers for these challenges and scare others away, which she viewed as a positive result. She explained, "You might scare some of them away, but there are some people that shouldn't be teaching." In addition, those might be the same teachers who would leave the profession within their first five years of teaching. In that respect, it would be better to allow them to choose a different career path while still in college.

Ms. Nelson also believed that the pre-service teachers who are committed to the teaching profession, like herself, would also benefit from being more aware of the challenges they might face as teachers. She explained, "I never heard the scary stuff." She added, "I didn't hear people come in and tell me that the parents were going to call me and blame me when their kid failed the class because their kid didn't do their homework."

She suggested pre-service teachers needed to hear the "real stories" from practicing teachers, so that they might be better prepared for their first year of teaching. She suggested, "A nice shot of reality in there would have been nice." She added, "It would be nice to hear from teachers who have that experience."

The interview with Ms. Nelson revolved around two major themes: realistic preparation and field experience. Ms. Nelson's primary frustration with her pre-service teacher education program was the overall lack of realistic preparation for all of the responsibilities of a teacher. She commented, "I just wasn't prepared for a lot of things." In her view, pre-service teacher education had failed her by not adequately preparing her for some of the most challenging aspects of her job, beyond simply planning or teaching a lesson.

According to Nelson, "Some of the stuff they just don't prepare you for, you know?" She mentioned several issues including classroom management, parents, and administration. Nelson explained, "I think there needs to be more preparation outside, for stuff dealing with the outside sources, but I've been saying that since I graduated and I got my job." By outside sources, Ms. Nelson was referring to everything outside of just teaching, such as dealing with students, parents, and administrators.

Another major theme in the interview with Ms. Nelson was the amount of field experience. During the interview, Ms. Nelson repeatedly expressed her concern about the amount of field experience in pre-service teacher education. She viewed the lack of field experience as a major weakness of her own pre-service teacher education program. In her experience, there was "not enough time in the real classroom." She added, "I would have benefited from spending more time [in the classroom]."

Ms. Nelson recommended that field experiences should begin earlier in the pre-service teacher education program. At one point in the interview, she commented, "Just start people out in the field earlier." In her view, this would have addressed a lot of the other issues for which she felt unprepared, such as classroom management and dealing with parents or administrators. At another point in the interview, she stated, "I think they [teacher educators] have to get them, they have to get us as students, in there right away." She recommended that field experiences should begin during the freshman year of the program.

Ms. Nelson began her postsecondary education at a community college where she spent time in a K–12 classroom during her freshman year. On the other hand, most of the other pre-service teachers in her university program did not spend any time in the classroom until their junior year. She felt fortunate that she was able to gain such valuable experience early in her education. This allowed her to experience the classroom at different grade levels and decide what grade level was the best fit for her abilities and interests. Based on her freshman field experience, she changed her major from elementary education to secondary science education.

Ms. Nelson also recommended two semesters of student teaching. In the interview, she explained that her student teaching experience felt "rushed." Nelson said, "I was only teaching a full day for a week." She also recommended that student teachers observe more teachers with varying levels of experience. She believed student teachers should observe "someone who's been teaching for thirty years [and] maybe someone who's been teaching for two." Why might this be beneficial? According to Nelson, "They're going to think in different ways and they might be able to give you more insight."

Ms. Nelson's emphasis on realistic preparation and field experience explains many of the other views she expressed in the survey and the interview. She strongly supported K–12 teaching experience for teacher educators and increased involvement for practicing teachers in pre-service teacher education. Her other recommendations for pre-service teacher education included decreasing the emphasis on topics such as multiculturalism, gender equity in science, and reading development. Conversely, she advocated for a greater emphasis on items that she considered more essential and practical, such as dealing with students, parents, and administration.

9

What Teachers Really Value in Teacher Education

The interviews with elementary and secondary teachers provided an opportunity for teachers to express their views on a variety of topics in pre-service teacher education. These conversations opened a window into the thoughts, perceptions, and beliefs of these eight teachers in a way that the surveys could not. The interviews also allowed the teachers to talk about other issues that concerned them and answer in ways that were not limited by a survey response form. In the interview, the teachers were better able to express the reasoning behind their views and make additional comments or suggestions regarding pre-service teacher education.

The views expressed during the interviews provided a second source of evidence for what teachers really think about pre-service teacher education. In this way, the interview data complemented and reaffirmed the findings of the survey. Because the teachers were purposively selected for the interview, they were able to share their insights about why teachers are satisfied or dissatisfied with pre-service teacher education. Likewise, they explained why they were willing or unwilling to become more involved.

Although the views of each individual teacher can provide valuable insights, the views and beliefs expressed by multiple teachers should be given more weight than a single comment or suggestion from a single teacher. In this chapter, the common views and beliefs from all of the interviews will be compared and discussed. Although the teachers each had unique experiences in pre-service teacher education, there were some remarkable similarities in the views they expressed during the interview.

Understanding these shared views and beliefs can be valuable for any teacher or teacher educator involved in pre-service teacher education. These shared values help us to better share the responsibility for preparing new teachers. So what do teachers really value in pre-service teacher education?

COMMON VIEWS OF TEACHERS

Each teacher was asked about the strengths and weaknesses of their pre-service teacher education experience during the interview. Many teachers expressed similar views in response to this question, as shown in table 9.1. The pseudonyms for the teachers are also listed in table 9.1 to show which teachers expressed each view.

The first four teachers listed are the teachers who were more satisfied with their pre-service teacher education experience: Foster, Wallace, Clark, and Cook. The second four teachers listed are the teachers who were less satisfied with their pre-service teacher education experience: Gray, Kraft, Ford, and Nelson. It is interesting to note that the teachers shared many common views about pre-service teacher education, regardless of their level of satisfaction. Although their opinions of pre-service teacher education varied, many of the teachers listed very similar strengths and weaknesses of pre-service teacher education.

Five of the eight teachers identified a good professor as the strength of their pre-service teacher education experience. In teacher education, we spend an enormous amount of time focused on the program curriculum and the assessment of pre-service teachers. We carefully select and sequence the courses that pre-service teachers will take in both the education department and content area departments.

The curriculum is carefully mapped out and aligned to state and national standards. Each credit is debated, reviewed, and revised to ensure that the program is meeting all of the requirements for accreditation and for the state review process. Likewise, teacher educators spend an enormous amount of time developing and implementing assessment systems, often meeting both state and accreditation requirements.

The simple and obvious message from teachers is that it was the professors that had the largest effect on their experience. This should not surprise

Table 9.1. Strengths and Weaknesses of Pre-service Teacher Education

Topic or Question	Common Views on Pre-service Teacher Education Expressed by Teachers During the Interviews	Satisfied Teachers				Dissatisfied Teachers			
		Foster	Wallace	Clark	Cook	Gray	Kraft	Ford	Nelson
Strengths of Teacher Education	Good Professor(s)					X		X	X
	Content Knowledge	X	X	X	X				
	Lesson Plans	X	X				X		
Weaknesses of Teacher Education	Classroom Management	X	X	X	X	X	X	X	X
	Idealistic Viewpoint			X	X	X	X	X	X
	Bad Modeling of Teaching			X		X	X		
	Bad Professor(s)			X		X	X		
	Not Prepared to be a Teacher						X	X	X
	Unrealistic Lesson Plans			X		X	X	X	X
	Not Age or Grade Level Specific	X	X					X	

anyone from the field of education. We all know the value and influence of an effective teacher, and yet we forget to emphasize this simple truth, that people matter most. If teacher educators spent more time connecting, advising, and mentoring pre-service teachers and less time revising curriculum and assessment systems, they could be more influential. Teaching will always be about the students, and these teachers have reminded us of that simple truth. Teacher education must also be student-centered.

The other two strengths of pre-service teacher education identified by the teachers during the interviews were content knowledge and lesson plans. Five of the eight teachers mentioned the development of content knowledge as a strength of their pre-service teacher education program. These teachers felt that they were well prepared to teach their content areas.

This is a compliment to the design of the pre-service program curriculum, the content area courses in the program, and the content area faculty who teach them. Finally, three of the eight teachers also identified lesson planning as a strength of their pre-service preparation. These teachers believed they were well prepared to plan effective lessons, as a result of the education coursework in their pre-service programs.

When asked about the weaknesses of their pre-service teacher education, eight of eight teachers identified classroom management. Similarly, classroom management was also identified on the survey as the number one issue for which teachers were unprepared. Although the teachers most often mentioned managing student behavior and discipline, some of the teachers also mentioned managing the facilities, equipment, paperwork, grading, and parent communication.

Research shows that this is a difficult skill for novice teachers to master. There is certainly a need for pre-service teacher education to address both theory and practices of classroom management. In addition, the pre-student teaching and student teaching field experiences provide students with opportunities to apply and refine their classroom management skills.

Another common weakness of pre-service teacher education identified by the teachers during the interviews was an overly idealistic portrayal of teaching. Five of the eight teachers believed that their pre-service preparation perpetuated an idealistic viewpoint of teaching and learning. These teachers felt blindsided by students who were not motivated to learn and parents who were quick to blame their teachers.

Some of the teachers interviewed also found it very difficult to plan lessons as they had been taught in pre-service teacher education. The time and budget constraints that exist in most schools had not been issues when planning lessons at the university. In fact, three of the eight teachers identified unrealistic lesson plans as one of the weaknesses of their pre-service program. These teachers believed that pre-service teachers needed to be more aware of the realistic conditions of schools, behavior of students, and responsibilities of the teacher.

While some of the teachers had identified a good professor as one of the strengths of their experience, three of the eight teachers identified a bad professor as one of the weaknesses. Furthermore, four of the eight teachers remarked that their education professors did a poor job of modeling the teaching practices they taught to the pre-service teachers. These teachers believed that modeling effective teaching practices was very important and needed to see each instructional strategy demonstrated to apply it more effectively in their own classrooms.

Finally, three of the eight also identified education courses that were not grade level specific as the weakness of their pre-service preparation. These teachers felt that the education courses would be better if they addressed the needs of one particular grade level, or at least were divided into separate elementary and secondary education courses.

COMMON RECOMMENDATIONS OF TEACHERS

The teachers were also given many opportunities to discuss and suggest recommendations for improving pre-service teacher education. The common recommendations made by the teachers during the interviews are shown in table 9.2. Once again, the pseudonyms for the teachers are provided in table 9.2. Many of these recommendations were also discussed earlier in chapter 6. The survey and interview showed very similar results in this regard, which demonstrated the reliability and validity of the findings.

The teachers made many recommendations for improving pre-service teacher education. First, all of the teachers who were interviewed recommended that teacher educators should be required to have experience in elementary or secondary schools. The teachers disagreed on whether this

Table 9.2. Common Recommendations for Pre-service Teacher Education

Topic or Question	Common Views on Pre-service Teacher Education Expressed by Teachers During the Interviews	Satisfied Teachers					Dissatisfied Teachers		
		Foster	Wallace	Clark	Cook	Gray	Kraft	Ford	Nelson
K–12 Experience for Teacher Educators	Required for Some or All Teacher Educators	X	X	X	X	X	X	X	X
	Required for ALL Teacher Educators	X		X	X	X	X	X	X
	Required for Teaching Methods Professors Only		X	X					
	Promotes a More Realistic Viewpoint	X		X	X	X	X	X	X
Teacher Involvement	Time is an Obstacle	X	X	X	X		X	X	X
	Would be More Practical and Realistic	X	X				X	X	X
	Would Improve Feedback and Communication	X	X	X			X	X	
	Would be Beneficial to Pre-service Teachers	X	X				X	X	
	Should be Guest Speakers More Often					X	X	X	X
	Would Share Real Experiences with Students			X		X	X	X	X
	Should Involve Retired Teachers	X	X		X				
More Field Experience	Need More Pre-student Teaching Experience	X	X			X	X	X	X
	Need More Student Teaching Experience				X	X	X	X	X
	Should Observe Multiple Teachers					X	X	X	X
Other Recommendations	More Realistic Preparation			X	X	X	X	X	X
	More on Classroom Management			X	X	X	X	X	X
	Less on History of Education					X	X	X	
	More Hands-on						X		
	More Content Preparation		X			X			X
	Less on Ed Psych					X		X	
	Less on Multiculturalism					X			X
	Less on Formal Lesson Plans			X			X		X

should apply to all teacher educators or only those who taught the teaching methods courses. Six of the eight teachers believed that it should apply to all teacher educators, regardless of the courses they teach. The other two teachers believed that only the professors who taught the teaching methods courses should be required to have K–12 experience. Five of the eight teachers believed that this would promote a more realistic perspective on teaching and learning.

Second, five of the eight teachers believed that involving elementary and secondary teachers more in pre-service teacher education would also bring a more practical and realistic perspective. Five of the eight teachers also believed that more teacher involvement would improve the communication and feedback loop between teachers and teacher educators. In addition, four of the teachers believed that teachers should be invited on campus as guest speakers, four of the teachers believed that teachers would be able to share real experiences from the classroom, and four of the teachers believed this would benefit pre-service teachers.

However, six of the eight teachers mentioned that time was the biggest obstacle to involving elementary and secondary teachers in pre-service teacher education. They mentioned things like young children at home and coaching, which made it very difficult to become more involved in pre-service teacher education at the university. The reasons were different for each teacher, but the common thread was that teachers lead very busy lives.

Some of the teachers mentioned their being at the school until late in the evening fulfilling their teaching and coaching duties. Although not all of the teachers were able to be involved, the teachers generally supported involving teachers and their ideas more. Three of the teachers suggested that retired teachers would be an ideal market to involve in pre-service teacher education. Retired teachers would have a more flexible time schedule to be able to spend time at the university and could act as mentors to the pre-service teachers.

Third, seven of the eight teachers interviewed recommended that pre-service teachers spend more time engaged in field experiences. These included both pre-student teaching and student teaching experiences. Four of the teachers recommended more pre-student teaching experiences, which could be offered throughout a four year pre-service program. This would help pre-service teachers learn and develop gradually over time.

In the field, the pre-service teachers would be able to apply what they had learned in the university classroom. In the university classroom, the experiences in the field would provide an authentic context to allow pre-service teachers to connect educational theory and practices to a first-hand experience.

Four of the teachers also recommended more student teaching, which was also found in the survey. Finally, three of the teachers believed that observing multiple teachers would benefit pre-service teachers more than one extended student teaching experience. This provided one rationale for including multiple pre-student teaching experiences in a pre-service teacher education program.

Fourth, the teachers offered several recommendations on the final question of the interview, which asked if the teachers had any other recommendations for pre-service teacher education. The most common responses related to a need for more practical preparation as well as more attention to the issue of classroom management. Six of the eight teachers expressed a need for pre-service teacher education to become more practical or realistic. This was consistent with the results of the survey, where teachers identified the need for more practical preparation as the number one dissatisfaction with current preparation.

Similarly, six of the eight teachers also recommended that more attention needed to be given to classroom management, including practical strategies that teachers can use to manage their time, workload, resources, and especially their students. This was also consistent with the results of the survey. When teachers in the survey were asked if there was anything for which they felt unprepared, the most common response was classroom management.

This was also mentioned by the teachers during the interview as one of the major weaknesses of their own pre-service teacher education experience. The need for more practical preparation and more attention to classroom management issues and strategies was a common view of most teachers. The teachers as a whole were quite adamant about these two recommendations during the interviews.

Finally, the teachers also suggested that pre-service teacher education should spend less time on topics such as the history of education, educational psychology, multiculturalism, and formal lesson plans. It seems that the teachers tended to consider these courses, and the concepts taught in these courses, as more abstract and theoretical. These were the elements of pre-service teacher education that they perceived as less practical.

One might take this recommendation literally to reduce the attention to these issues in pre-service teacher education. However, an alternative explanation and course of action may be more prudent. These courses need to become more practical and focus more on how teachers can apply these ideas in real and practical ways. If teachers fail to see the connection between these ideas and their practice, then the manner in which these topics are typically taught should be thoughtfully and reflectively reviewed by teachers and teacher educators.

Conversely, the teachers suggested that pre-service teacher education should spend more time on content area preparation and hands-on activities. These suggestions also reflect the teachers' emphasis on courses and strategies that could be considered less abstract and more practical, especially to a beginning teacher. This point of emphasis may help teacher educators make every course and experience in pre-service teacher education more meaningful and effective.

COMMON BELIEFS OF TEACHERS

In addition to the individual views expressed, several themes emerged from each teacher interview. The themes reflect the core beliefs and values of the teachers interviewed. The themes were ideas that each teacher emphasized throughout the interview at multiple times and in response to multiple questions. The themes also provide a means to interpret and explain many of the other views expressed by the teachers in both the interview and the survey.

A summary of the individual themes from each teacher interview can be seen in table 9.3. The pseudonyms of each teacher are also provided in table 9.3. The themes derived from each individual interview help to identify central ideas that were especially important to the teachers, including those who were generally satisfied and those who were generally dissatisfied with their pre-service experience. Collectively, the common themes provide insight into what teachers really value in pre-service teacher education.

Table 9.3. Individual Themes from Teacher Interviews

Individual Themes	Satisfied with Teacher Education				Dissatisfied with Teacher Education			
	Ms. Foster	Ms. Wallace	Mr. Clark	Mr. Cook	Mr. Gray	Ms. Kraft	Mr. Ford	Ms. Nelson
Realistic Preparation			X	X	X	X		X
Field Experience		X			X	X		X
Classroom Management			X				X	
Content Preparation		X			X			
Professors							X	
Group Psychology			X					
Professionalism				X				
Respect				X				
Unprepared Student Teachers	X							

Realistic preparation and field experience were the most common themes that emerged from the interviews with practicing teachers on pre-service teacher education. Five of the eight teachers interviewed, emphasized the need for realistic preparation of pre-service teachers in pre-service teacher education, throughout their interviews. Four of the eight teachers interviewed emphasized the field experience component as they discussed a variety of topics in pre-service teacher education.

Collectively, these two themes were especially important to the teachers interviewed and provide a valuable insight into the perspective of in-service teachers on pre-service teacher education. Only Mr. Ford and Ms. Foster did not emphasize at least one of these topics during their interviews. For the other teachers, it was a fairly common battle cry for teacher education reform.

The theme of realistic preparation was the most common theme identified in the eight interviews with practicing teachers. The type of realistic preparation that the teachers called for was often set in contrast to the perceived idealism of pre-service teacher education programs and faculty. The teachers perceived pre-service teacher education as being quite idealistic about student motivation, behavior, and learning.

In his interview, Mr. Cook described pre-service teacher education as "too philosophical" and "too cerebral." Mr. Gray discussed specifically how the methods and lesson plans taught in pre-service teacher education were different from what was typically done, or even possible, in the field. These teachers felt that pre-service teacher education needed to present preparation that was more practical and pragmatic. They believed that the more realistic preparation would help new teachers be more successful and effective in the classroom, especially during the first few years of teaching.

The second theme of field experience was very much interconnected to teachers' beliefs about the practicality of pre-service teacher education. Because they believed that much of what was taught in pre-service teacher education was impractical, they valued field experience more highly than the university-based classroom experience. From their perspective, the field experience allowed them to learn the practical lessons that the university classroom could not teach them.

For this reason, teachers called for more field experience throughout the pre-service teacher education program. They believed more pre-student teaching experiences would provide more opportunity for hands-on experiences and better preparation for student teaching. Likewise, increasing the length of the student teaching experience could allow students to learn the practical lessons to prepare them for teaching.

The two most common themes identified by the interview analysis, realistic preparation and field experience, provided a useful framework for understanding and interpreting many of the views expressed by teachers in the survey and interviews. In short, practicing teachers favored a more pragmatic approach to the training of teachers emphasizing those things that would have a more immediate effect on pre-service teachers and help a beginning teacher first cope and then succeed in the classroom. The interview themes revealed a commonly held belief system of the teachers interviewed and provided a lens for interpreting the survey and interview results.

The views and recommendations of teachers expressed on the survey and described earlier in this book are consistent with the common themes that emerged from the interviews. In chapters 4 and 5, teachers expressed the following views on pre-service teacher education:

- Nearly half of teachers believed that their pre-service teacher education experience was somewhat (34 percent), mostly (12 percent), or very (1 percent) irrelevant.
- Some teachers felt mostly (13 percent) or very (2 percent) unprepared for their first year of teaching. When asked what they felt unprepared for, the most common response was classroom management.
- One out of four teachers were mostly (22 percent) or very (3 percent) unsatisfied with current pre-service teacher education. When asked to explain their rating of current pre-service teacher education, the most common response was the need for more practical preparation.
- Nearly half of teachers believed there was a significant (42 percent) or very significant (3 percent) gap between what is taught in education courses and what is practiced.
- Two out of three teachers were probably (50 percent) or definitely (16 percent) in favor of their own school becoming a professional development school, where universities and K–12 schools create strong connections and partnerships.

In chapter 6, teachers supported the following recommendations for pre-service teacher education:

- The most popular recommendation from teachers was to increase the amount of field experience. Four out of ten teachers recommended more than one semester of student teaching. In the interview, the teachers also supported multiple pre-student teaching experiences with multiple teachers.
- The second most popular recommendation from teachers was to provide more practical preparation. In addition, the number one dissatisfaction expressed by teachers in the survey was the need for more practical preparation.
- Many teachers recommended that more time should be devoted to classroom management (86 percent of teachers), content area (42 percent of teachers), and teaching methods (40 percent of teachers) courses. The more practical and concrete nature of these courses may explain the high value teachers place on these courses.
- Some teachers recommended that less time be devoted to educational psychology (18 percent of teachers) and school in society (17 percent) courses. These courses may have been considered more abstract and theoretical by teachers.
- Most teachers recommended that teacher educators should probably (29 percent) or definitely (67 percent) be required to have experience in elementary or secondary schools.
- Most teachers also recommended that teacher educators should probably (43 percent) or definitely (43 percent) be encouraged to return to teach at the K–12 level periodically during the tenure as education professors.
- Most teachers recommended that elementary and secondary teachers should probably (55 percent) or definitely (30 percent) be more involved in pre-service teacher education.

These views and recommendations are indicative of the teachers' strongly held beliefs in a pragmatic approach to pre-service teacher education. The terms idealistic, unrealistic, cerebral, theoretical, and philosophical were all used by various teachers to depict and criticize the perceived ivory tower nature of pre-service teacher education. Practicing teachers believed a pragmatic approach to pre-service teacher education could best be achieved through a combination of realistic university-based preparation and ample field experience. This is what teachers value the most in teacher education.

10

Points to Remember

This book began by presenting a rationale for why teachers should be consulted on the current issues and reforms that dominate the dialogue in the field of teacher education. Research has shown that when faculty in schools of education have presented views and strategies that are consistent with those of elementary and secondary teachers in the field, pre-service teachers are more likely to accept, adopt, and apply those views and strategies (Tatto, 1996). To be consistent views, may require an exchange of ideas about how new teachers can best be prepared for the classroom.

This does not suggest that teachers' views should replace those of teacher educators. Rather, it suggests that teachers can add a perspective that complements the more theoretical and research-based perspective of teacher educators. As teacher educators recognize the practical concerns and constraints of teachers, they are better able to convey research and theory in the context of practice so it has meaning and value to a nineteen-year-old pre-service teacher. When this occurs, pre-service teachers are more likely to use the research and theory to inform their practice.

Although this has been known for some time, the views of teachers have not been well researched or represented in the academic literature of teacher education (Toll, Nierstheimer, Lenski, & Kolloff, 2004). The views of practicing teachers, and the depth of experience and knowledge they possess as practitioners, is largely an untapped resource for research in teacher education. The possibility for future research that involves the perspective of in-service teachers is genuinely limitless. If pre-service teachers are to construct meaning from educational research and theory, it must be presented through the lens of practice. It must be meaningful and authentic.

Throughout the book, you have been immersed in the thoughts of practicing teachers on their own pre-service teacher education experience and the state of current pre-service teacher education. In the preceding chapters, you have read about their concerns and recommendations. You have seen pre-service teacher education through the lens of practicing teachers. What have we learned? How can we process and apply what we have learned to improve our efforts to prepare the next generation of teachers?

LEVEL OF SATISFACTION

The overall satisfaction of teachers with their pre-service preparation was quite good. Despite the many complaints and criticisms often heard from individuals on the condition and status of pre-service teacher education, four out of five teachers reported a positive experience. One in five teachers rated their experience as poor or fair. Likewise, most teachers found their pre-service teacher education experience to be relevant to the job of a teacher. Only one in ten described their pre-service preparation as mostly or very irrelevant. Later in the survey and interviews, however, the issue of relevance, or the practicality of pre-service preparation, was a concern expressed by many teachers.

Based on this evidence, one could argue that there is room for improvement in pre-service teacher education. Although teacher education is not broken, it could be better. The views expressed by teachers point to one area of potential reform. Teacher education must better address the practical issues and duties of teachers. This may lead teacher educators to question some of their curricula, in light of this finding.

It may also lead us to question how we measure and reflect on our effectiveness as teacher educators. Perhaps, the performance of a pre-service teacher on a portfolio review or interview is less important than their performance in the classroom with students. Perhaps, the feedback from teachers one year after they graduate is less important than their feedback five years after they graduate, when they have had more time to reflect on teaching and reflect on their pre-service preparation.

In the survey, the teachers identified multiple issues for which they felt unprepared, including:

- Classroom Management
- Workload
- Working with Parents
- Time Management
- Working with Administration
- Teaching Methods
- Curriculum
- Assessment
- Planning Lessons

The top five items on this list were issues that also were consistent with the two major themes of the interviews: realistic preparation and field experiences. Many teachers felt unprepared to assume all of the roles and responsibilities of a teacher in their first year. Although this may be true of many professionals, teaching is truly unique in its approach to starting new teachers. While other professions often ease new members into their new role, new teachers are typically given the same level of responsibilities as veteran teachers. In many cases, they may even be given a more difficult teaching assignment because seniority has allowed the veteran teachers to teach the preferred students or courses.

The survey indicated many issues for which teachers felt unprepared. Teacher educators take note. These practical issues and challenges must be addressed in the curriculum and instruction of pre-service teacher education, whether in a university-based course or field experience. Interestingly, most of the issues for which teachers felt unprepared may require skills that can only be practiced and mastered in the context of meaningful field experiences. This only reinforces the need for strong partnerships between schools and universities in preparing teachers.

Although teachers were generally satisfied with their own pre-service preparation, they rated their satisfaction with current pre-service teacher education slightly lower. The teachers provided the following reasons to explain their dissatisfaction with current pre-service teacher education:

- The need for more practical preparation
- Bad experiences with a student teacher(s)

- Shortages or shortcomings of field experiences
- Poor preparation in classroom management
- Too many hoops required for certification

Once again, these findings from the survey are consistent with the findings from the interviews, where the need for more realistic preparation and the need for more field experience were the two most common themes. It is also consistent with the perceived theory-practice gap between what is taught in pre-service teacher education and what is practiced in the elementary and secondary classroom. Nearly half of teachers believed there was a significant or very significant gap between theory and practice. This does not devalue educational theory. It only devalues the practice of teaching theory without multiple clear connections to practical applications for teaching and learning, as it occurs in real classrooms.

In other words, it is not the theory that is impractical; it is the presentation of theory apart from an authentic context that makes it appear impractical to pre-service teachers. As teacher educators, we must recognize the importance of presenting theory within an authentic context. We also need to ensure that pre-service teachers have had enough meaningful experiences in the classroom to understand and construct their own meaning when presented with concepts, research, and theory. This presents a challenge and opportunity for teachers and teacher educators involved in pre-service teacher education.

DIFFERENCES BASED ON SUBJECT AREA

We also learned that the responses of teachers varied significantly based on gender and subject area on multiple questions. In general, teachers in the language arts were significantly more positive and more willing to become involved in pre-service teacher education than teachers in math and science. There were four instance of differences based on subject area:

- Teachers of technology education, music, foreign language, and English as a second language rated the relevance of their pre-service teacher education experience significantly higher than teachers of social studies, math, and science.

- Teachers in music, foreign language, and English as a second language were also more willing to become involved in pre-service teacher education as guest speakers or guest teachers than teachers of social studies, math, and science.
- Teachers of English, foreign language, and English as a second language were more willing to become involved as full-time university instructors of education courses than teachers in math, science, or technology education.
- Teachers in music, English, and multiple subjects were more likely than teachers in social studies, math, and technology education to believe that having K–12 teachers teach university education courses would be beneficial.

These differences based on subject areas could be a reflection of some differences in the learning needs or styles of pre-service teachers based on subject area. Perhaps, the curriculum and instruction in pre-service teacher education is catered more toward those with a gift and interest in language or auditory learning. Perhaps, pre-service teachers in science, technology, engineering, and mathematics are not well served by the typical approaches taken in pre-service teacher education, which often emphasize course readings followed by class discussions and written papers.

In this respect, pre-service teacher education could learn from the pedagogies of science, technology, engineering, and mathematics (STEM), which emphasize experiential learning, problem solving, and using evidence to form explanations and arguments. In education courses, pre-service teachers could be asked to identify a research question or problem, collect information, collect observations in the field, and interpret their findings based on the evidence collected.

This approach to teacher education would fit nicely within a teacher education program that provides students with ample field experiences, effectively ties field experiences to coursework, and promotes reflection and evidence-based practices among pre-service teachers. These approaches to teacher education may better serve the needs of all pre-service teachers, especially those in science, technology, engineering, and mathematics (STEM) who are currently less satisfied and less willing to become involved in pre-service teacher education.

DIFFERENCES BASED ON GENDER

In addition, we also learned that females consistently rated pre-service teacher education higher than their male counterparts in response to multiple questions on the survey. The analysis of the results showed that the differences were statistically significant. Females rated the following items on the survey higher than males:

- Quality of their pre-service teacher education experience
- Relevance of their pre-service teacher education experience
- Satisfaction with current pre-service teacher education
- Support of professional development schools
- Support of standards-based approaches to teacher education
- Willingness to meet with teacher educators
- Willingness to guest teach in pre-service teacher education courses
- Willingness to teach pre-service teacher education courses part-time
- Expanding the amount of time devoted to teaching methods courses

Although the survey did not reveal a reason, it did reveal a statistically significant gender difference on multiple items. For whatever reason, females generally have a better experience and perception of pre-service teacher education than males. There may be something about pre-service teacher education that meets the needs of women to a greater degree than men. In a female dominated profession, perhaps these results should not be a surprise. It should, however, be a concern for teachers and teacher educators.

This result is also consistent with the differences noted earlier based on subject area. If you recall, teachers in the language arts generally reported a more positive experience in pre-service teacher education and were more willing to become involved than teachers in math or science. In general, there are more male teachers in math and science than in the language arts. These teachers may not be as gifted as auditory or linguistic learners, and may instead prefer more kinesthetic or scientific approaches to knowing and learning.

As mentioned previously, a common approach to pre-service teacher education courses emphasizes course readings followed by class discussions and written papers. This is a heavily linguistic approach to teaching and learning, and may be better suited to the learning styles of women, in general. As we know, females often demonstrate slightly higher abilities in reading and language than males on a variety of different standardized measures. In contrast, men in general may benefit more from an experiential and evidence-based approach to pre-service teacher education. Of course, this is just one hypothesis that is yet to be tested.

There may be many other hypotheses to explain these findings as well. In the same way that university programs in science, technology, engineering, and mathematics (STEM) may unknowingly convey a bias against women, there could be a hidden bias against men in the field of education. If so, what is it about teaching or pre-service teacher education that leaves men more dissatisfied with their professional preparation? This is an important question that has yet to be answered. You may have your own hypothesis to test and explore.

More research is needed to explain why men are generally less satisfied with pre-service teacher education than women. While the need for more women in the STEM fields is well documented and researched, the same cannot be said about the need for more men in education. In addition to more research, the recruitment, retention, and support of men in education through grant dollars, scholarships, or specialized programs should be implemented, as it has with women in the STEM fields.

Given the growing absenteeism of fathers, male teachers have a vital role to play in the emotional and sociological development of school-aged children, both boys and girls. According to the U.S. Census Bureau, one in three children in the United States lives in a home without their biological father (2011). Research suggests that these children are at a higher risk for poverty, emotional and behavioral problems, teen pregnancy, drug use, juvenile delinquency, and incarceration (Bush, Mullis, & Mullis, 2000; Harper & McLanahan, 2004; Hoffmann, 2002; Osborne & McLanahan, 2007; Teachman, 2004; U.S. Census Bureau, 2011). One research study also found that when fathers are more involved at school, the academic achievement of children is higher (Nord & West, 2001).

At a time when there are fewer fathers in the home, we should be striving to put more men in the classroom. While a male teacher can never replace a father, the involvement of men in the lives of young people is certainly influential. The social and emotional benefits of a positive male role model can be quite important. Teacher education must find ways to recruit and retain this underrepresented population of teachers and better serve their needs as they prepare for the profession. Similarly, teacher educators must thoughtfully reflect on their own practices and how they might affect men differently than women.

FINAL RECOMMENDATIONS

We also learned what teachers really want to change about teacher education. Many of the teachers' recommendations logically stemmed from the list of items for which they felt unprepared and the reasons for their dissatisfaction with pre-service teacher education. Recall, the number one dissatisfaction of teachers with current pre-service teacher education was the perceived lack of practical preparation. Based on the survey and interview results, teachers recommended and supported the following changes to pre-service teacher education:

- More pre-student teaching and student teaching field experiences
- More practical preparation
- More on classroom management, content area, and teaching methods
- Less on history of education, educational psychology, and multiculturalism
- Requiring elementary or secondary experience for teacher educators
- Encouraging teacher educators to periodically return to K–12 teaching
- More teacher involvement in teacher education

This list of recommendations highlights the need for teacher education to be more realistic and practical. Teachers recommended more pre-student teaching and student teaching field experience for pre-service teachers and more K–12 experience for teacher educators because they believed this would result in more practical and effective preparation. The educational courses or topics the teachers valued most—classroom management, content area, and teaching methods—were the topics with the most obvious practical connections to the daily roles and responsibilities of the teacher.

The educational courses or topics with less obvious applications—history of education, educational psychology, and multiculturalism—were not highly valued by teachers. If the applications of these courses and concepts are not evident to the veteran teacher, we should not be surprised that the veteran teacher would not value the experience. Furthermore, if the applications of these concepts are not evident to the veteran teacher, how much more abstract must they seem to pre-service teachers, who have much less classroom experience.

Another way that teachers recommended changing pre-service teacher education was to involve practicing teachers in a variety of different ways. This is also a strategy for bringing a more practical perspective to university pre-service teacher education programs and courses. Based on the survey, nearly nine out of ten teachers believed that elementary and secondary teachers and their ideas should be more involved in pre-service teacher education. The teachers were willing to become involved in pre-service teacher education in the following ways:

- Meeting with faculty members (seven out of ten teachers)
- Guest teaching or speaking (six out of ten teachers)
- Teaching part-time (five out of ten teachers)
- Teaching full-time for one year (five out of ten teachers)

These teachers were willing to become involved in ways that extended well beyond the traditional role of the cooperating teacher. Because they also supported the periodic return of teacher educators to K–12 classrooms, many teachers supported the idea of a teacher-faculty exchange program as well. While most teachers would accept a salary as compensation for teaching part-time or full-time, many others would consider using graduate credits or a reduction in K–12 teaching duties as compensation. These options could give schools of education more flexibility to design courses and find instructors in creative ways, which given the current budgetary restrictions, could be valuable.

The teachers who were interviewed believed that more teacher involvement would improve feedback and communication between teachers and teacher educators, allow K–12 teachers to share real experiences with students, and bring a more practical or realistic perspective to the university pre-service teacher education courses. During the interviews, many teachers identified time as the largest obstacle for increased teacher involvement. Teachers simply do not have time to add additional responsibilities, without taking something away. As a potential solution to this problem, some teachers suggested that retired teachers should become more involved in pre-service teacher education.

In response to these findings, teacher educators might benefit from viewing each course and each course topic through the lens of the practicing teacher. If the applications of educational concepts or theories are not clear and evident to the pre-service teachers, then they will not benefit from the course, nor will they be able to apply what they have learned in the course to their practice. The lens of the practicing teacher provides a new opportunity to examine each practice and reform in teacher education.

The message to all teachers and teacher educators who work with pre-service teachers is two-fold. First, teachers and teacher educators must work collaboratively to improve the preparedness of beginning teachers. Second, pre-service teachers need to see clear examples and applications of research and theory in every university course and field experience. As teachers and teacher educators move toward evidence-based practice, teacher educators cannot teach the evidence and practice independently, and expect novices in the profession to connect the dots.

FINAL THOUGHTS

In this book, you read about the views of teachers and met eight teachers who cared deeply about teaching and teacher education, enough to respond to a survey and participate in an interview on their own time. These eight teachers were real people, with real personal and professional lives. In their personal and professional lives, they faced challenges and struggles. Teaching and teacher education has many challenges, but it also has many rewards.

Most teachers enter the teaching profession for a combination of the following three reasons: they love working with kids, they love the subjects they teach, and they think they can make a valuable contribution to an individual and a society through teaching. These teachers reflected those characteristics and ambitions. They wanted to make a difference in both the education of their students and the education of pre-service teachers.

Even those who were not satisfied with pre-service teacher education, and in some cases were very critical of their own experiences and current practices, were willing to respond to a survey and meet for an interview to share their thoughts and beliefs. These conversations revealed what teachers value in pre-service teacher education and what from their own experience affected them the most.

The survey and interviews shed light on the views and opinions of in-service teachers on a wide variety of topics. The perspective of in-service teachers has been nearly absent in the research literature on teacher education. The survey results provided a collection of mostly descriptive statistics on teachers' views on topics in pre-service teacher education as well as some significant inferential statistics.

The interviews revealed many themes, which revealed the core beliefs and values of the teachers interviewed. The themes from the interviews included:

- Realistic Preparation
- Field Experience
- Classroom Management
- Content Preparation
- Professors
- Group Psychology
- Professionalism
- Respect
- Unprepared Student Teachers

In their discussion of pre-service teacher education, these were the issues that teachers returned to time and time again. The themes from each individual interview revealed a lot about each individual teacher. More importantly, the common themes that emerged across multiple interviews, revealed what teachers really value in pre-service teacher education. By far, the most common themes were realistic preparation and field experience.

The type of realistic preparation that teachers called for was often set in contrast to the perceived idealism of pre-service teacher education programs and faculty members. Because these teachers believed that a portion of what was taught in pre-service teacher education was impractical, they valued field experience more highly than the university-based experience. Realistic preparation and field experience are what teachers really value and what they believe will positively affect pre-service teachers the most.

Although they offered both praises and criticisms of pre-service teacher education, most teachers had a positive experience in pre-service teacher education. More importantly, they cared deeply about teaching and teacher education. The overall message to teacher educators is one of collaboration and partnership. Teachers are very interested and willing to get involved in teacher education in a wide variety of ways. The barriers that divide teachers and teacher educators may be slowly eroding. The communication and collaboration that have emerged provide promise for the future of teaching and teacher education.

The theoretical framework and models for engaging teachers as partners in pre-service teacher education already exist. Teacher educators have opportunities to engage teachers through advisory boards, professional learning communities, professional organizations, and professional development schools, and many already take advantage of these systems to some extent. Teacher educators must use the systems already in place to form meaningful partnerships with teachers and to utilize their insights and involvement to continually imrpove pre-service teacher education.

The English philosopher Francis Bacon famously said, "Knowledge is power," but truly knowledge is only power when it has been applied to affect an individual or society. This book has generated new knowledge. It has conveyed the views and recommendations of elementary and secondary teachers on a variety of topics in pre-service teacher education. Although much more research is needed, the voices of teachers provide a new perspective on the effectiveness and practicality of current practices in teacher education. These insights may help teachers and teacher educators to partner together to better prepare the next generation of teachers for success and longevity in the classroom.

It is up to those involved in pre-service teacher education to ultimately use this knowledge and evidence to inform their own practice. Just as teacher educators encourage pre-service teachers to become reflective practitioners, so too must we reflect on our own practice based on the evidence available to us. The views of practicing teachers provide us with an opportunity to reflect. The power of education is reflected in the ability of students to apply their new knowledge. If we apply what we have learned from teachers, then Francis Bacon was right. Knowledge is power.

Appendix A

Teacher Survey Instrument

Name_____

Teacher Survey:
The Views of Practicing Teachers on Pre-service Teacher Education

---

Background Information

Age _____   School _____

Gender (M/F) _____   Number of Years of Teaching
                           Experience _____

Race_____   Number of Years Since Initial
                           Certification _____

Grade Level(s) _____   Number of Graduate Credits _____

Subject(s) _____   Degree(s) Earned _____

_____   _____

1. What type of pre-service teacher education program did you attend? (Circle One)
   Traditional Undergraduate Master's Degree Alternative Certification Other

2. What is the name of the university or organization where you did your pre-service teacher education training? _____
   _____

3. Please provide a basic description of your pre-service teacher education program:

   _____
   _____
   _____
   _____
   _____

The purpose of this survey is to investigate the views of practicing teachers on a variety of topics in pre-service teacher education including the potential for greater teacher involvement in pre-service teacher educa-

tion. If you are unfamiliar with any of the vocabulary found in the survey, a glossary of terms is located on the final page of the document.

Section One: Assessing Your Pre-service Teacher Education Experience

1. How would you rate your overall *pre-service teacher education experience*? (Circle One)

1	2	3	4	5
Poor	Fair	Good	Very Good	Excellent

2. How relevant was your *pre-service teacher education* experience to the practice of teaching? (Circle One)

1	2	3	4	5
Very Irrelevant	Mostly Irrelevant	Somewhat Relevant	Mostly Relevant	Very Relevant

3. How well prepared were you to teach in your first year of teaching? (Circle One)

1	2	3	4	5
Very Unprepared	Mostly Unprepared	Somewhat Prepared	Mostly Prepared	Very Prepared

What, if anything, were you not prepared for in your first year?

4. How much did your teaching methods during your student teaching reflect what was taught in your university methods course? (Circle One)

1	2	3	4	5
None	A Little	Some	A lot	All

5. How much do your current teaching methods reflect what was taught in your university methods course? (Circle One)

1	2	3	4	5
None	A Little	Some	A lot	All

Section Two: Assessing Current Pre-service Teacher Education

6. How satisfied are you with the quality of current *pre-service teacher education* programs? (Circle One)

1	2	3	4	5
Very	Mostly	No	Mostly	Very
Unsatisfied	Unsatisfied	Opinion	Satisfied	Satisfied

Why or why not?

7. In your opinion, how significant, if at all, is the gap between what is taught in current teacher education methods courses and what is practiced in K – 12 classrooms? (Circle One)

1	2	3	4	5
No	An	No	A	A Very
Gap	Insignificant	Opinion	Significant	Significant
at All	Gap		Gap	Gap

Section Three: Cooperating Teachers

8. Have you ever been a cooperating teacher? (Circle One)

    Yes   or   No

    If yes, how many student teachers have you had as a cooperating teacher? _____

9. How informed are you on the practices of your local *pre-service teacher education* program(s)? (Circle One)

1	2	3	4	5
Very	Mostly	Somewhat	Mostly	Very
Uninformed	Uninformed	Informed	Informed	Informed

10. As a cooperating teacher, would you be willing to allow a student teacher to try instructional methods that are different from your own? (Circle One)

1	2	3	4	5
Not	Only	Some	Most	All
at All	a Little	of the Time	of the Time	of the Time

Section Four: Extended Field Experience

11. How many semesters of student teaching did you teach in your *pre-service teacher education* program? _____

12. How many semesters of student teaching should be included in *pre-service teacher education*? _____

Section Five: Professional Development Schools (See Glossary)

13. Have you ever taught in a *professional development school* ?

    Yes   or   No

14. Would you be in favor of your school becoming a *professional development school* in collaboration with a nearby university? (Circle One)

1	2	3	4	5
Definitely	Probably	No	Probably	Definitely
Not	Not	Opinion	Yes	Yes

Section Six: Standards-based Teacher Education (See Glossary)

15. Do you support a *standards-based* approach to *pre-service teacher education*? (Circle One)

1	2	3	4	5
Definitely	Probably	No	Probably	Definitely
Not	Not	Opinion	Yes	Yes

16. Should course grades, portfolios, or both be used to assess a pre-service teachers' satisfactory completion of a teacher education program? (Circle One)

    Course Grades   Portfolios   Both   No Opinion

Section Seven: Alternative Teacher Certification Options (See Glossary)

17. Should college graduates with a bachelor's degree in their field and eight weeks of summer training in education be certified to teach? (Circle One)

1	2	3	4	5
Definitely	Probably	No	Probably	Definitely
Not	Not	Opinion	Yes	Yes

18. Should college graduates with a bachelor's degree in their field and no formal training in education be certified to teach? (Circle One)

1	2	3	4	5
Definitely	Probably	No	Probably	Definitely
Not	Not	Opinion	Yes	Yes

19. Do you believe *pre-service teacher education* programs should be at the undergraduate level (bachelor's degree), graduate level (master's degree), or both? (Circle One)

    Undergraduate Level   Graduate Level   Both   No Opinion

Section Eight: Teaching Experience for Teacher Educators

20. Should university teacher education faculty members be required to have K – 12 teaching experience prior to employment as an education professor? (Circle One)

1	2	3	4	5
Definitely	Probably	No	Probably	Definitely
Not	Not	Opinion	Yes	Yes

    If so, how many years of teaching experience should be required?
    _____

21. Should university teacher education faculty members be encouraged to return to K – 12 classrooms to teach periodically during their tenure as education professors? (Circle One)

1	2	3	4	5
Definitely	Probably	No	Probably	Definitely
Not	Not	Opinion	Yes	Yes

If so, how often should they return to the classroom? Every _____ years.

Section Nine: Involving Practicing Teachers in Teacher Education

22. Should practicing teachers and their ideas be more involved and influential in *pre-service teacher education*? (Circle One)

1	2	3	4	5
Definitely	Probably	No	Probably	Definitely
Not	Not	Opinion	Yes	Yes

23. Have you ever met with faculty members from a college or university to discuss the teacher education program? (Circle One)

Yes   or   No

24. Would you be willing to meet with faculty from a college or university to discuss the teacher education program? (Circle One)

1	2	3	4	5
Definitely	Probably	Maybe	Probably	Definitely
Not	Not		Yes	Yes

25. Assuming they could be scheduled, how much, if at all, would regular meetings between practicing teachers and university education faculty members benefit or improve teacher education? (Circle One)

1	2	3	4	5
Not at All	Slightly	Somewhat	Quite	Very
Beneficial	Beneficial	Beneficial	Beneficial	Beneficial

26. Have you ever taught or co-taught an education course at a college or university? (Circle One)

    Yes   or   No

27. Would you be willing to occasionally guest teach or co-teach a university education course for a day if the university paid for a substitute teacher? (Circle One)

1	2	3	4	5
Definitely Not	Probably Not	Maybe	Probably Yes	Definitely Yes

28. Assuming it could be arranged, would you be willing to teach or co-teach a university education course on a regular basis as a part-time instructor? (Circle One)

1	2	3	4	5
Definitely Not	Probably Not	Maybe	Probably Yes	Definitely Yes

    If maybe, probably yes, or definitely yes, which of these three forms of compensation would you accept? (Circle one or more answers)

1	2	3
Graduate credits from the university	A part-time instructor's salary from the university	A reduction in K–12 teaching duties

29. Would you be willing to teach or co-teach university education courses as a full-time visiting faculty member for one year if you were paid your current teaching salary and benefits and guaranteed to return to your previous K – 12 teaching duties the following year? (Circle One)

1	2	3	4	5
Definitely Not	Probably Not	Maybe	Probably Yes	Definitely Yes

Do you support teacher-faculty exchange programs where teachers teach or co-teach university education courses full-time while university faculty members teach in the K–12 classroom for one year? (Circle One)

1	2	3	4	5
Definitely Not	Probably Not	No Opinion	Probably Yes	Definitely Yes

30. Assuming it could be arranged, how much, if at all, would having practicing teachers teach or co-teach university education courses benefit or improve teacher education? (Circle One)

1	2	3	4	5
Not at All Beneficial	Slightly Beneficial	Somewhat Beneficial	Quite Beneficial	Very Beneficial

Section Ten: Recommendations for Teacher Education

31. Should the amount of time devoted to **content area courses** in *pre-service teacher education* be reduced, expanded, or stay the same? (Circle One)

1	2	3
Reduced	Expanded	Stay the Same

32. Should the amount of time devoted to **methods courses** in *pre-service teacher education* be reduced, expanded, or stay the same? (Circle One)

1	2	3
Reduced	Expanded	Stay the Same

33. Should the amount of time devoted to **classroom management** in *pre-service teacher education* be reduced, expanded, or stay the same? (Circle One)

1	2	3
Reduced	Expanded	Stay the Same

34. Should the amount of time devoted to the **role of school in society** in *pre-service teacher education* be reduced, expanded, or stay the same? (Circle One)

    1   2   3
    Reduced   Expanded   Stay the Same

35. Should the amount of time devoted to **educational psychology** in *pre-service teacher education* be reduced, expanded, or stay the same? (Circle One)

    1   2   3
    Reduced   Expanded   Stay the Same

36. What other comments or suggestions, if any, do you have for *pre-service teacher education* programs? (Add an additional sheet if necessary)

Following the survey, I will be selecting 10-15 teachers to interview in order to gain a better understanding of the reasoning behind some of the views expressed in this survey.

Are you willing to be interviewed?   Yes   or   No

If yes, please provide your phone number and email address below.

PhoneNumber:_____ Email:_____

Glossary of Terms

Teacher education: the education of teachers for the purposes of acquiring knowledge, understanding, and skills in the field of education before and after initial certification.

Pre-service teacher education: the education of teachers before their initial certification and employment as a teacher.

In-service teacher education: the education of teachers after their initial certification and during their teaching careers.

Standards-based teacher education: an approach to teacher education that uses a set of standards to describe the knowledge, abilities and skills that pre-service teachers must demonstrate in order to be certified to teach.

Professional development school: an elementary, middle, or high school that has formed a partnership with a university teacher education program to improve student achievement, teacher effectiveness, and teacher education.

Alternative teacher certification: the initial certification of teachers through any approach other than traditional university undergraduate teacher education programs.

Teacher-centered teaching method: a teaching method where the teacher is the primary focal point of the classroom.

Student-centered teaching method: a teaching method where student activity is the primary focal point of the classroom.

Appendix B

Teacher Interview Instrument

Name _____

Date _____

Teacher Interview
The Views of Practicing Teachers on Teacher Education

Background Information

Age _____	Years of Teaching Experience _____
Gender _____	Number of Years Certified _____
Race _____	University of Certification _____
Subject _____	Number of Graduate Credits _____
_____	Degree(s) Earned _____
Grade Level(s) _____	_____

The following interview will be conducted as a semi-structured interview. The questions below will guide the discussion. Other topics and questions may be pursued in order to follow up on the particular thoughts and views expressed by the teacher being interviewed.

Opening Question
1. (Show the teacher a copy of their survey and allow a few minutes). What did you think of the issues raised in the survey?

Section One: Assessing Your Pre-service Teacher Education Experience
2. You rated your pre-service teacher education experience as _____ (in question one of the survey). Could you explain why?
3. What were the strengths or the most valuable aspects of your teacher education program? OR What courses or experiences in teacher education were most beneficial?
4. What were the weakness or least valuable aspects of your teacher education program? OR What courses or experiences in teacher education were least beneficial?

Section Two: Assessing Current Pre-service Teacher Education

5. You said that you were _____ with current pre-service teacher education (in question 6 of the survey). Why did you say that?
6. Upon what did you base your assessment of current pre-service teacher education?
7. What areas are student teachers or new teachers generally most proficient? Least proficient?
8. You said that there was _____ between what is taught in current teacher education methods courses and what is practiced (in question 7 of the survey). Could you explain why?

Section Three: Cooperating Teachers

9. Should cooperating teachers be more informed about the university-based courses and curriculum? In what ways? How would it help?
10. Should cooperating teachers be more involved in the university teacher education? In what ways?

Section Four: Extended Field Experience

11. You suggested _____ semesters of student teaching (in question 12 of the survey). Could you explain why you suggested that number? How might that help teacher preparation?

Section Five: Professional Development Schools

12. You _____ support your school becoming a professional development school (question 14 of the survey). Could you explain why?
13. What can teachers or teacher educators do to make professional development schools highly effective?

Section Six: Standards-based Teacher Education

14. You _____ standards-based teacher education? What do you like or not like about it?

Section Seven: Alternative Certification

15. You suggested that teacher education programs be offered at the _____ level (in question 19 of the survey). Why do you feel that way?

Section Eight: Teaching Experience for Teacher Educators

16. You said that teacher education faculty _____ have K–12 teaching experience (in question 20 of the survey). Why? Should it be required or recommended?

17. Do you think that applies to professors who teach the methods course or professors who teach any education course?

Section Ten: Involving Teachers in Teacher Education

18. You responded that practicing teachers _____ be more involved in pre-service teacher education (question 22 of the survey). Why do you feel that way?

19. You said that you _____ meet regularly with teacher educators (in question 24 of the survey). Could you explain why?

20. You also said that you _____ be willing to teach or co-teach a university education course on a regular basis (in question 28 of the survey). Why?

21. How might having practicing teachers more involved in teacher education benefit teacher education, if at all?

22. Do you have other ideas for how practicing teachers might become more involved in teacher education?

Recommendations for Teacher Education

23. What aspects of teaching or learning to teach are overemphasized in pre-service teacher education? Why?

24. What aspects of teaching or learning to teach are underemphasized in pre-service teacher education? Why?

25. What are the important characteristics of an effective program in teacher education?

26. What could be done in teacher education to ease the transition from the university to the first several years of teaching?

27. Do you have any other recommendations for teacher education or teacher educators?

Appendix C

Teacher Survey Results

SECTION ONE: ASSESSING YOUR
PRE-SERVICE TEACHER EDUCATION EXPERIENCE

Question 1:	1 Poor	2 Fair	3 Good	4 Very Good	5 Excellent
How would you rate your overall pre-service teacher education experience?	9 4.8% N = 189	31 16.4% Mean = 3.39	59 31.2% Std Dev = 1.10	57 30.2% Median = 3	33 17.5% Mode = 3

Question 2:	1 Very Irrelevant	2 Mostly Irrelevant	3 Somewhat Relevant	4 Mostly Relevant	5 Very Relevant
How relevant was your pre-service teacher education experience to the practice of teaching?	2 1.1% N = 189	23 12.2% Mean = 3.49	64 33.9% Std Dev = 0.88	80 42.3% Median = 4	20 10.6% Mode = 4

Question 3:	1 Very Unprepared	2 Mostly Unprepared	3 Somewhat Prepared	4 Mostly Prepared	5 Very Prepared
How well prepared were you to teach in your first year of teaching?	3 1.6% N = 190	25 13.2% Mean = 3.43	74 38.9% Std Dev = 0.93	64 33.7% Median = 3	24 12.6% Mode = 3

	1 None	2 A Little	3 Some	4 A Lot	5 All
Question 4: How much did your teaching methods during your student teaching reflect what was taught in your university methods course?	3 1.6% N = 189	33 17.5% Mean = 3.13	93 49.2% Std Dev = 0.78	56 29.6% Median = 3	4 2.1% Mode = 3
Question 5: How much do your current teaching methods reflect what was taught in your university methods course?	1 None 16 8.6% N = 186	2 A Little 59 31.7% Mean = 2.69	3 Some 79 42.5% Std Dev = 0.87	4 A Lot 31 16.7% Median = 3	5 All 1 0.5% Mode = 3

SECTION TWO: ASSESSING CURRENT
PRE-SERVICE TEACHER EDUCATION

Question 6:	1	2	3	4	5
How satisfied are you with the quality of	Very Unsatisfied	Mostly Unsatisfied	No Opinion	Mostly Satisfied	Very Satisfied
current pre-service teacher education programs?	5 2.7%	40 22.0%	53 29.1%	76 41.8%	8 4.4%
	N = 182	Mean = 3.23	Std Dev = 0.94	Median = 3	Mode = 4
Question 7:	1	2	3	4	5
	No Gap at All	An Insignificant Gap	No Opinion	A Significant Gap	A Very Significant Gap
In your opinion, how significant, if at all, is the					
gap between what is taught in current teacher education methods courses and what is practiced in K–12 classrooms?	2 1.1%	38 21.0%	60 33.1%	76 42.0%	5 2.8%
	N = 181	Mean = 3.24	Std Dev = 0.85	Median = 3	Mode = 4

SECTION THREE: COOPERATING TEACHERS

Question 8:
Have you ever been a cooperating teacher?

	Yes	No	
	98	93	
	51.3%	48.7%	
	N = 191		

If yes, how many student teachers have you had as a cooperating teacher?

N = 94			
Mean = 4.28	Std Dev = 3.61	Median = 3.75	Mode = 1.00	Range = 14.00

Question 9:
How informed are you on the practices of your local pre-service teacher education program(s)?

1 Very Un-informed	2 Mostly Un-informed	3 Somewhat Informed	4 Mostly Informed	5 Very Informed
35	44	57	38	8
19.2%	24.2%	31.3%	20.9%	4.4%
N = 182	Mean = 2.67	Std Dev = 1.14	Median = 3	Mode = 3

Question 10:
As a cooperating teacher, would you be willing to allow a student teacher to try instructional methods that are different from your own?

1 Not at All	2 Only a Little	3 Some of the Time	4 Most of the Time	5 All of the Time
0	4	39	91	43
0%	2.3%	22.0%	51.4%	24.3%
N = 177	Mean = 3.98	Std Dev = 0.75	Median = 4	Mode = 4

SECTION FOUR: EXTENDED FIELD EXPERIENCE

	0-0.25 semester	0.50 semester	1.00 semester	1.25-1.75 semesters	2.00 semesters	2.50-4.00 semesters
Question 11: How many semesters of student teaching did you teach in your pre-service teacher education program? _____	5 2.6% N = 190	16 8.4% Mean = 1.04	154 81.1% Std Dev = 0.46	1 0.5% Median = 1.00	10 5.3% Mode = 1.00	4 2.1% Range = 4.00
Question 12: How many semesters of student teaching should be included in pre-service teacher education? _____	1 0.5% N = 183	2 1.1% Mean = 1.45	103 56.3% Std Dev = 0.68	17 9.2% Median = 1.00	49 26.8% Mode = 1.00	11 6.0% Range = 4.00

Note: Questions 11 and 12 were asked using a fill in the blank format. The responses were placed into the numerical categories above for the purpose of reporting frequency.

SECTION FIVE: PROFESSIONAL DEVELOPMENT SCHOOLS

Question 13: Have you ever taught in a professional development school?	Yes	No		
	22	164		
	11.8%	88.2%		
	N = 186			

Question 14: Would you be in favor of your school becoming	1 Definitely Not	2 Probably Not	3 No Opinion	4 Probably Yes	5 Definitely Yes
a professional development school in collaboration with a nearby university?	2	17	45	93	30
	1.1%	9.1%	24.1%	49.7%	16.0%
	N = 187	Mean = 3.71	Std Dev = 0.88	Median = 4	Mode = 4

SECTION SIX: STANDARDS-BASED TEACHER EDUCATION

Question 15: Do you support a standards-based approach to pre-service teacher education?	1 Definitely Not	2 Probably Not	3 No Opinion	4 Probably Yes	5 Definitely Yes
	6	16	32	99	35
	3.2%	8.5%	17.0%	52.7%	18.6%
	N = 188	Mean = 3.75	Std Dev = 0.96	Median = 4	Mode = 4

Question 16: Should course grades, portfolios, or both be used to assess a pre-service teachers' satisfactory completion of a teacher education program?	Course Grades	Portfolios	Both	No Opinion
	22	7	139	20
	11.7%	3.7%	73.9%	10.6%
	N = 188			

SECTION SEVEN: ALTERNATIVE
TEACHER CERTIFICATION OPTIONS

Question 17:	1	2	3	4	5
Should college graduates	Definitely	Probably	No	Probably	Definitely
with a bachelor's degree	Not	Not	Opinion	Yes	Yes
in their field and eight					
weeks of summer	61	91	11	24	0
training in education be	32.6%	48.7%	5.9%	12.8%	0%
certified to teach?					
	N = 187	Mean = 1.99	Std Dev = 0.95	Median = 2	Mode = 2

Question 18:	1	2	3	4	5
	Definitely	Probably	No	Probably	Definitely
Should college graduates	Not	Not	Opinion	Yes	Yes
with a bachelor's					
degree in their field and	141	43	3	3	0
no formal training in	74.2%	22.6%	1.6%	1.6%	0%
education be certified to					
teach?					
	N = 190	Mean = 1.31	Std Dev = 0.58	Median = 1	Mode = 1

Question 19:	Under-	Graduate	Both	No	
Do you believe	graduate	Level		Opinion	
pre-service teacher	Level				
education programs					
should be at the	72	4	105	7	
undergraduate level	38.3%	2.1%	55.9%	3.7%	
(bachelor's degree),					
graduate level (master's					
degree), or both?					
	N = 188				

SECTION EIGHT: TEACHING EXPERIENCE FOR TEACHER EDUCATORS

Question 20:
Should university teacher education faculty be required to have K – 12 teaching experience prior to employment as an education professor?

1 Definitely Not	2 Probably Not	3 No Opinion	4 Probably Yes	5 Definitely Yes
1	5	2	56	127
0.5%	2.6%	1.0%	29.3%	66.5%
N = 191	Mean = 4.59	Std Dev = 0.70	Median = 5	Mode = 5

If so, how many years of teaching experience should be required? _____

1.0-2.5 years	3.0-3.5 years	4.0-4.5 years	5.0-5.5 years	6.0-9.5 years	10-20 years
9	37	13	74	14	27
5.1%	21.2%	7.5%	42.5%	8.1%	15.5%
N = 174	Mean = 5.45	Std Dev = 2.74	Median = 5.0	Mode = 5.0	Range = 19.0

Question 21:
Should university teacher education faculty members be encouraged to return to K – 12 classrooms to teach periodically during their tenure as education professors?

1 Definitely Not	2 Probably Not	3 No Opinion	4 Probably Yes	5 Definitely Yes
2	15	11	81	81
1.1%	7.9%	5.8%	42.6%	42.6%
N = 190	Mean = 4.18	Std Dev = 0.93	Median = 4	Mode = 4.5

If so, how often should they return to the classroom? Every _____ years.

1.0-2.5 years	3.0-3.5 years	4.0-4.5 years	5.0-5.5 years	6.0-9.5 years	10.0 years
19	23	7	78	16	13
12.2%	14.7%	4.5%	50.0%	10.2%	8.3%
N = 156	Mean = 4.97	Std Dev = 2.12	Median = 5.0	Mode = 5.0	Range = 9.0

Note: The second part of questions 20 and 21 were asked using a fill in the blank format. The responses were placed into numerical categories for the purpose of reporting frequency.

SECTION NINE: INVOLVING PRACTICING TEACHERS IN TEACHER EDUCATION

	1 Definitely Not	2 Probably Not	3 No Opinion	4 Probably Yes	5 Definitely Yes
Question 22: Should practicing teachers and their ideas be more involved and influential in pre-service teacher education?	0 0% N = 190	6 3.2% Mean = 4.12	22 11.6% Std Dev = 0.73	105 55.3% Median = 4	57 30.0% Mode = 4

Question 23: Have you ever met with faculty members from a college or university to discuss the teacher education program?	Yes 60 31.6%	No 130 68.4%	N=190		

	1 Definitely Not	2 Probably Not	3 Maybe	4 Probably Yes	5 Definitely Yes
Question 24: Would you be willing to meet with faculty from a college or university to discuss the teacher education program?	1 0.5% N = 190	11 5.8% Mean = 3.94	43 22.6% Std Dev = 0.90	79 41.6% Median = 4	56 29.5% Mode = 4

	1 Not at All Beneficial	2 Slightly Beneficial	3 Somewhat Beneficial	4 Quite Beneficial	5 Very Beneficial
Question 25: Assuming they could be arranged, how much, if at all, would regular meetings between practicing teachers and university faculty members benefit or improve teacher education?	2 1.1% N = 186	17 9.1% Mean = 3.67	50 26.9% Std Dev = 0.89	88 47.3% Median = 4	29 15.6% Mode = 4

Question 26:	Yes	No		
Have you ever taught or				
co-taught an education	18	173		
course at a college or	9.4%	90.6%		
university?				
	N = 191			

Question 27:	1	2	3	4	5
	Definitely	Probably	Maybe	Probably	Definitely
Would you be willing to	Not	Not		Yes	Yes
occasionally guest teach					
or co-teach a university	5	33	42	56	55
education course for a	2.6%	17.3%	22.0%	29.3%	28.8%
day if the university paid					
for a substitute teacher?					
	N = 191	Mean	Std Dev	Median	Mode = 4
		= 3.64	= 1.15	= 4	

Question 28:	1	2	3	4	5
Assuming it could be	Definitely	Probably	Maybe	Probably	Definitely
arranged, would you	Not	Not		Yes	Yes
be willing to teach or					
co-teach a university	12	39	51	46	40
education course on a	6.4%	20.7%	27.1%	24.5%	21.3%
regular basis as a part-					
time instructor?					
	N = 188	Mean	Std Dev	Median	Mode = 3
		= 3.34	= 1.21	= 3	

If maybe, probably yes,	1	2	3
or definitely yes, which	Graduate	A part-time	A reduction in k-12
of these three forms of	credits	instructor's salary	teaching duties
compensation would		from the univ.	
you accept? (Circle one	73	129	62
or more answers)	51.0%	90.2%	43.4%
	N = 143		

Question 29:	1 Definitely Not	2 Probably Not	3 Maybe	4 Probably Yes	5 Definitely Yes
Would you be willing to teach or co-teach university education courses as a full-time visiting faculty member for one year if you were paid your current teaching salary and benefits and guaranteed to return to your previous K – 12 teaching duties the following year?	13 6.9%	40 21.2%	51 27.0%	36 19.0%	49 25.9%
	N = 189	Mean = 3.36	Std Dev = 1.26	Median = 3	Mode = 3

Question 30:	1 Definitely Not	2 Probably Not	3 No Opinion	4 Probably Yes	5 Definitely Yes
Do you support teacher-faculty exchange programs where teachers teach or co-teach university education courses full-time while university faculty members teach in the K–12 classroom for one year?	0 0%	22 11.5%	31 16.2%	97 50.8%	41 21.5%
	N = 191	Mean = 3.82	Std Dev = 0.90	Median = 4	Mode = 4

Question 31:	1 Not at All Beneficial	2 Slightly Beneficial	3 Somewhat Beneficial	4 Quite Beneficial	5 Very Beneficial
Assuming it could be arranged, how much, if at all, would having practicing teachers teach or co-teach university education courses benefit or improve teacher education?	2 1.1%	14 7.5%	44 23.5%	86 46.0%	41 21.9%
	N = 187	Mean = 3.80	Std Dev = 0.90	Median = 4	Mode = 4

SECTION TEN: RECOMMENDATIONS FOR TEACHER EDUCATION

		1 Reduced	2 Expanded	3 Stay the Same
Question 32: Should the amount of time devoted to **content area courses** in pre-service teacher education be reduced, expanded, or stay the same?	N = 187	9 4.8%	79 42.2%	99 52.9%
Question 33: Should the amount of time devoted to **methods courses** in pre-service teacher education be reduced, expanded, or stay the same?	N = 189	19 10.1%	76 40.2%	94 49.7%
Question 34: Should the amount of time devoted to **classroom management** in pre-service teacher education be reduced, expanded, or stay the same?	N = 187	1 0.5%	161 86.1%	25 13.4%
Question 35: Should the amount of time devoted to the **role of school in society** in pre-service teacher education be reduced, expanded, or stay the same?	N = 182	31 17.0%	54 29.7%	97 53.3%
Question 36: Should the amount of time devoted to **educational psychology** in pre-service teacher education be reduced, expanded, or stay the same?	N = 190	35 18.4%	51 26.8%	104 54.7%

References

Abdal-Haqq, I. (1998). *Professional development schools: Weighing the evidence.* Thousand Oaks, CA: Corwin Press.

Adelman, N.E. (1986). *An exploratory study of teacher alternative certification and retraining programs.* Washington, DC: Policy Studies Associates, Inc.

American College Testing (ACT). (2011). *ACT Profile Report-National: Graduating Class 2011.* Retrieved from http://www.act.org/newsroom/data/2011/pdf/profile/National2011.pdf

Book, C.L. (1996). Professional development schools. In J. Sikula, T.J. Buttery, & E. Guyton (Eds.), *Handbook of research on teacher education* (pp. 194–210). New York: Macmillan.

Boyle-Baise, M., & McIntyre, D.J. (2008). What kind of experience? Preparing teachers in PDS or community settings. In M. Cochran-Smith, S. Feiman-Nemser, D.J. McIntyre, & K.E. Demers (Eds.), *Handbook of research on teacher education: Enduring questions in changing contexts* (pp. 307–29). New York and London: Routledge, Taylor, and Francis Group.

Bush, C., Mullis, R., & Mullis, A. (2000, August). Differences in empathy between offender and nonoffender youth. *Journal of Youth and Adolescence, 29,* 467–78.

Calderhead, J., & Shorrock, S. (1997). *Understanding teacher education.* London: Falmer.

Charters, W.W., & Waples, D. (1929). *Commonwealth teacher training study.* Chicago: University of Chicago Press.

Clarke, S.C.T. (1969). The story of elementary teacher education models. *Journal of Teacher Education, 20(3),* 283–93.

Clifford, G.J., & Guthrie, J.W. (1988). *Ed school: A brief for professional educa-*
tion. Chicago: University of Chicago Press.

Cochran-Smith, M., & Lytle, S.L. (1992). *Inside/Outside: Teacher research and*
knowledge. New York: Teachers College Press.

Darling-Hammond, L. (Ed.;1994a). *Professional development schools: Schools*
for developing a profession. New York: Teachers College Press.

Darling-Hammond, L. (1994b). Who will speak for the children? How Teach for
America hurts urban schools and students. *Kappan, 76(1),* 21–34.

Darling-Hammond, L. (1999). *Reshaping teaching policy, preparation, and prac-*
tice. Influences of the National Board for Professional Teaching Standards.
Washington, DC: American Association of Colleges for Teacher Education.

Darling-Hammond, L., Wise, A., & Klein, S. (1995). *A license to teach: Building*
a profession for the 21st-century schools. Boulder, CO: Westview.

Darling-Hammond, L., Wise, A., & Klein, S. (1999). Licensing teachers: The
need for change. In *A license to teach: Raising standards for teaching* (pp.
1–15). San Francisco: Jossey Bass.

Denzin, N.K., & Lincoln, Y.S. (2000). *Handbook of qualitative research* (2nd
ed.). Thousand Oaks, CA: Sage Publications.

Dewey, J. (1929). The sources of a science of education. In J.A. Boydston (Ed.),
John Dewey: The latter works (1984). Carbondale: Southern Illinois University.

Dill, V.S. (1996). Alternative teacher certification. In J. Sikula, T.J. Buttery, &
E. Guyton (Eds.), *Handbook of research on teacher education* (pp. 932–60).
New York: Macmillan.

Ewing, R., & Smith, D.L. (2002). Building communities in teacher education:
The M.Teach. experience. In H. Christiansen & S. Ramadevi (Eds.), *Reedu-*
cating the educator: Global perspectives on community building (pp. 151–69).
Albany, NY: SUNY Press.

Feistritzer, C.E. (1985). *The condition of teaching: A state by state analysis.*
Princeton, NJ: The Carnegie Foundation for the Advancement of Teaching.

Feistritzer, C.E. (1999). *The making of a teacher: A report on teacher prepara-*
tion in the US. Washington, DC: National Center for Educational Information.

Feistritzer, C.E. (2005). *Profile of alternate route teachers.* Washington, DC:
National Center for Education Information.

Feistritzer, C.E. (2008). *Alternative teacher certification: A state by state analysis*
2007. Washington, DC: National Center for Educational Information.

Feistritzer, C.E., & Haar C.K. (2008). *Alternative routes to teaching.* Upper
Saddle River, NJ: Pearson Education.

Fenstermacher, G. (1990). The place of alternative certification in the education
of teachers. *Peabody Journal of Education, 67(3),* 155–85.

Fleener, C. (1999). *Teacher attrition: Do PDS programs make a difference?* A paper (Distinguished Dissertation in Education Award winner) presented at the annual meeting of the Association of Teacher Educators, Chicago, IL.

Fox, J.E. (2006). Job-sharing in a boundary-spanning role: A professor returns to the classroom. In K.R. Howey & N.L. Zimpher (Eds.), *Boundary Spanners* (pp. 211–36). Washington, DC: American Association of State Colleges and Universities.

Glickman, C., & Bey, T. (1990). Supervision. In W.R. Houston (Ed.), *Handbook of research on teacher education.* New York: Macmillan.

Gold, Y. (1996). Beginning teacher support: Attrition, mentoring, and induction. In J. Sikula, T.J. Buttery, & E. Guyton (Eds.), *Handbook of research on teacher education* (pp. 548–94). New York: Macmillan.

Gordon, M. (2008). Between constructivism and connectedness. *Journal of Teacher Education, 59(4)*, 322–31.

Greenwood, A.M. (2003). Factors influencing the development of career-change teachers' science teaching orientation. *Journal of Science Teacher Education, 14(3)*, 217–34.

Grossman, P.L., & Loeb, S. (2008). *Alternative routes to teaching: Mapping the new landscape of teacher education.* Cambridge, MA: Harvard Education Press.

Grossman, P.L., Valencia, S.W., Evans, K., Thompson, C., Martin, S., & Place, N. (2000). Transitions into teaching: Learning to teach writing in teacher education and beyond. *Journal of Literacy Research, 32(4)*, 631–62.

Haberman, M. (1996). Selecting and preparing culturally competent teachers for urban schools. In J. Sikula, T.J. Buttery, & E. Guyton (Eds.), *Handbook of research on teacher education* (pp. 747–60). New York: Macmillan.

Hallinan, M.T., & Khmelkov, V.T. (2001). Recent developments in teacher education in the United States of America. *Journal of Education for Teaching, 27(2)*, 175–85.

Harper, C., & McLanahan, S. (2004, Septemeber). Father absence and youth incarceration. *Journal of Research on Adolescence, 14*, 369–97.

Hite, H. (1973). The cost of performance-based teacher education. *Journal of Teacher Education, 24*, 224.

Hoffmann, J. (2002, May). The community context of family structure and adolescent drug use. *Journal of Marriage and Family, 64*, 314–30.

Holmes Group. (1990). *Tomorrow's schools: Principles for the design of professional development schools.* East Lansing, MI: Holmes Group.

Holmes Group (1995). *Tomorrow's schools of education.* East Lansing, MI: Holmes Group.

Houston, W.R., Hollis, L.Y., Clay, D., Ligons, C.M., & Roff, L. (1999). Effects of collaboration on urban teacher education programs and professional development schools. In D. Byrd & J. McIntyre (Eds.), *Research on professional development schools. Teacher education yearbook VII* (pp. 29–45). Thousand Oaks, CA: Corwin.

Huling, L. (1998). *Early field experiences in teacher education.* East Lansing, MI: National Center for Research on Teacher Learning.

Humphrey, D.C., & Wechsler, M.E. (2007). Insights into alternative certification: Initial findings from a national study. *Teachers College Record,* 109(3), 483–530.

Joyce, B., Howey, K., & Yarger, S. (1977). *Pre-service teacher education.* Palo Alto: Booksend Laboratory.

Kennedy, M.M. (2005). *Inside teaching: How classroom life undermines reform.* Cambridge, MA: Harvard University Press.

Kopp, W. (1994). *An analysis of "Who will speak for the children?"* Unpublished memo distributed within Teach for America. New York: Teach for America.

Kornfeld, J., Grady, K., Marker, P., & Ruddell, M. (2007). Caught in the current: A self-study of state-mandated compliance in a teacher education program. *Teachers College Record, 109(8),* 1902–930.

Kraft, N. (2001). *Standards in teacher education: A critical analysis of NCATE, INTASC, and NBPTS.* Seattle, WA: American Educational Research Association.

Labaree, D.F. (2004). *The trouble with ed schools.* New Haven and London: Yale University Press.

Lehane, C.S. (2008). The democratic take. *Education Next, 8(1),* 56–59.

Lee, O., & Yarger, S.J. (1996). Modes of inquiry in research on teacher education. In J. Sikula, T.J. Buttery, & E. Guyton (Eds.), *Handbook of research on teacher education* (pp. 14–37). New York: Macmillan.

Levine, M. (2002, March). Why invest in professional development schools? *Educational Leadership,* 65–68.

Levine, A. (2006). *Educating school teachers.* Washington, DC: Education Schools Project.

Lucas, C. (1996). *Teacher education in America.* New York: St. Martin's Press.

Martin, A., Munby, H., & Hutchinson, N. (1998). *Protest and praise from the field: Focus groups and predictive validity.* Paper presented at the Canadian Society for the Study of Education, Ottawa.

McBee, R.H., & Moss, J. (2002, March). PDS partnerships come of age. *Educational Leadership,* 61–64.

McCullick, B.A. (2001). Practitioners' perspectives on values, knowledge, and skills needed by PETE participants. *Journal of Teaching in Physical Education, 21,* 35–56.

McDonald, F. (1973). Behavior modification and teacher education. In C. Thoresen (Ed.), *Behavior modification in education* (pp. 41–76). Chicago: University of Chicago Press.

National Center for Education Statistics. (NCES, 1999). *National Study of Post-secondary Faculty (NSOPF)*. Washington, DC: U.S. Department of Education.

National Center for Education Statistics. (NCES, 2008). *Fast Facts: Teacher Trends*. Retrieved from http://nces.ed.gov/fastfacts/display.asp?id=28.

National Center for Education Statistics. (NCES, 2011). *Digest of Education Statistics 2011*. Retrieved from http://nces.ed.gov/programs/digest/d11/tables/dt11_286.asp.

National Commission on Excellence in Education. (1983). *A nation at risk: The imperative for educational reform*. Washington, DC: Government Printing Office.

National Commission on Teaching and America's Future. (1996). *What matters most: Teaching for America's future*. New York: National Commission on Teaching for America's Future.

Nord, C., & West, J. (2001). *Fathers' and mothers' involvement in their children's schools by family type and resident status*. Washington, DC: U.S. Department of Education, National Center for Education Statistics.

Perry, B., Dockett, S., Kember, T., & Kuscher, K. (1999). Collaboration between schools and universities in early childhood teacher education. *Teaching in Higher Education, 4(3),* 383–97.

Petrie, H.G. (Ed.;1995). *Professionalization, partnership, and power: Building professional development schools*. Albany, NY: State University of New York Press.

Post, L.M., Pugach, M.C., Harris S., & Hedges, M. (2006). The teachers-in-residence program: Veteran urban teachers as teacher leaders in boundary-spanner roles. In K.R. Howey & N.L. Zimpher (Eds.), *Boundary Spanners* (pp. 211–36). Washington, DC: American Association of State Colleges and Universities.

Richardson-Koehler, V. (1988). Barriers to the effective supervision of student teaching: A field study. *Journal of Teacher Education, 39(2),* 28–34.

Sandefur, J.T., & Nicklas, W.L. (1981). Competency-based teacher education in AACTE institutions. *Phi Delta Kappan, 62,* 747–48.

Schlechty, P., & Vance, V. (1983). Recruitment, selection, and retention: The shape of the teaching force. *The Elementary School Journal, 83(4),* 469–87.

Shaker, P. (2001). "Teacher testing: A symptom." Washington, DC: U.S. Department of Education. (ERIC Document Reproduction Service No. SP 039578)

Sharpe, T.L. (1992). Teacher preparation—A professional development school approach. *Journal of Physical Education, Recreation, and Dance, 63,* 82–87.

Sharpe, T.L., Bahls, V., Lounsbery, M., Wolfe, P., Brown, M., Golden, C., & Deibler, C. (1995). Tips for beginning a collaborative activity: Three case studies. *Journal of Physical Education, Recreation, and Dance, 66(4),* 22–24, 55–57.

Sharpe, T.L., Bahls, V., Wolfe, P., Seagren, S., Brown, M., & Deibler, C. (1994). Tips for collaborating: How K–12 and university professionals can work together. *Strategies, 8,* 5–9.

Shulman, L.S. (1986). Those who understand: Knowledge growth in teaching. *Educational Researcher, 15(2),* 4–14.

Stallings, J.A. (1991). *Connecting pre-service teacher education and in-service professional development: A professional development school.* Paper presented at the annual meeting of the American Educational Research Association, Chicago.

Stallings, J.A., & Kowalski, T. (1990). Research on professional development schools. In W.R. Houston, M. Haberman, & J. Sikula (Eds.), *Handbook of research on teacher education* (pp. 251–63). New York: Macmillan.

Stoddart, T., & Floden, R.E. (1989). *School district-based teacher training: An alternative route to teacher certification.* Paper presented at the annual meeting of the American Educational Research Association, San Francisco.

Storz, M. (2003). Students' advice to prospective middle school teachers: Learning from the experiences of future students. *Teacher Education and Practice, 16(1),* 71–83.

Tatel, E. (1999). Teaching in under-resourced schools: The Teach for America example. *Theory into Practice, 38(1),* 37–45.

Tatto, M.T. (1996). Examining values and beliefs about teaching diverse students: Understanding the challenges for teacher education. *Education Evaluation and Policy Analysis, 18(2),* 155–80.

Teachman, J. (2004, January). The childhood living arrangements of children and the characteristics of their marriages. *Journal of Family Issues, 25,* 86–111.

Teitel, L. (1997). Changing teacher education through professional development school partnerships: A five-year follow-up study. *Teachers College Record, 99(2),* 311–334.

Teitel, L. (2003). *The professional development school handbook.* Thousand Oaks, CA: Corwin Press.

Toll, C.A., Nierstheimer, S.L., Lenski, S.D., & Kolloff, P.B. (2004). Washing our students clean: Internal conflicts in response to pre-service teachers' beliefs and practices. *Journal of Teacher Education, 55(2),* 164–76.

United States Census Bureau. (2011). *Children's living arrangements and characteristics: March 2011.* Washington, DC.

Upitis, R. (1999). Teacher education reform: Putting experience first. *Teacher Education Quarterly, 26(2),* 11–20.

Valli, L., Cooper, D., & Frankes, L. (1997). Professional development schools and equity: A critical analysis of rhetoric and research. *Review of Research in Education, 22,* 251–304.

Wait, D.B. (2000). *Are professional development school trained teachers really better?* Paper presented at the annual meeting of the National PDS Conference, Columbia, SC.

Wilson, S.M., Floden, R.E., & Ferrini-Mundy, J. (2002). Teacher preparation research: An insider's view from the outside. *Journal of Teacher Education, 53(3)*, 190–204.

Wise, A.E., & Darling-Hammond, L. (1987). *Licensing teachers: Design for a teaching profession.* Santa Monica, CA: RAND Corporation.

Zeichner, K. (2003). The adequacies and inadequacies of three current strategies to recruit, prepare, and retain the best teachers for all students. *Teacher College Record, 105(3)*, 490–519.

Zeichner, K., & Hoeft, K. (1996). Teacher socialization for cultural diversity. In J. Sikula, T.J. Buttery, & E. Guyton (Eds.), *Handbook of research on teacher education* (pp. 525–47). New York: Macmillan.

Zeichner, K., & Hutchinson, E. (2008). The development of alternative certification policies and programs in the United States. In P. Grossman & S. Loeb (Eds.), *Alternative routes to teaching: Mapping the new landscape of teacher education* (pp. 15–30). Cambridge, MA: Harvard Education Press.

Zionts, L., Shellady, S., & Zionts, P. (2006). Teachers' perceptions of professional standards: Their importance and ease of implementation. *Preventing School Failure, 50(3)*, 5–12.

Zumwalt, K. (1996). Simple answers: Alternative teacher certification. *Education Researcher, 25(8)*, 40–44.

About the Author

Kevin O. Mason is an associate professor in the School of Education at the University of Wisconsin-Stout in Menomonie, Wisconsin. Since 2006, he has served as the program director for science education at the University of Wisconsin-Stout. He previously held positions as a chemistry and physics teacher at Chippewa Falls High School and Middleton High School in Wisconsin. He lives in Chippewa Falls, Wisconsin, with his wife Emily and four children: Haley, Esubalew, Solomon, and Gubgnit.

CPSIA information can be obtained at www.ICGtesting.com
Printed in the USA
BVOW05s0558200814

363461BV00002B/7/P